TOMMY McINALLY

Celtic's Bad Bhoy?

TOMMY McINALLY

Celtic's Bad Bhoy?

David Potter

Black & White Publishing

First published 2009
by Black & White Publishing Ltd
29 Ocean Drive, Edinburgh EH6 6JL

1 3 5 7 9 10 8 6 4 2   09 10 11 12 13

ISBN: 978 1 84502 260 0

A CIP catalogue record for this book is available
from the British Library.

The publisher has made every reasonable effort to contact copyright
holders of images in the picture section. Any errors are inadvertent
and anyone who, for any reason, has not been contacted is invited
to write to the publisher so that a full acknowledgment can be
made in subsequent editions of this work.

Typeset by RefineCatch Limited, Bungay, Suffolk
Printed and bound by MPG Books Ltd, Bodmin

Contents

Dedication

And ithers, like your humble servant,
Poor wights! Nae rules nor roads observin',
To richt or left eternal swervin',
   They zig-zag on;
Till curst with age, obscure an' starvin'
   They aften groan

Robert Burns – 'Epistle to James Smith'

Acknowledgements

My thanks go to the relatives of Tommy McInally who helped me in my researches – notably Tom McInally, Michael McInally and Tom Higgins. Ian Stewart was also helpful with details of the McInally family. Fellow Celtic supporters Tom Campbell, Craig McAughtrie, Marie Rowan, Pat Woods and George Sheridan were also very encouraging and indeed were my fellow travellers on the Joseph Rafferty Celtic Supporters Bus in Kirkcaldy. My late friend John Jolly was very helpful too, as were Richard Grant and John McCue. Thanks also to the many supportive and professional people in the National Library of Scotland, Dundee's Wellgate Library and Sunderland Public Library.

Two men above all others must be singled out, sadly neither of them with us any more. One was the prolifically erudite Eugene MacBride who bequeathed me his 'fascicles' – an account of every game that Celtic ever played along with comments in his own inimitable style. The other was my own father Angus Potter who watched Tommy McInally many times and talked about him endlessly.

1

Who Was He?

The name Tommy McInally is heard less often these days. This is hardly surprising for he died more than fifty years ago. His very name however had a ring to it. It was frequently heard coming from the old Parkhead 'Jungle' in the dreadful days of the late 1950s and early 1960s when the earnest young forwards, not without talent and application but ill-directed by management which combined the worst of fecklessness and dictatorship, were repeatedly reminded that they were not as good as Patsy Gallacher and Tommy McInally. When a young fan would show his appreciation for the fine play of Steve Chalmers, Charlie Gallagher or John Divers, the older ones would look at him patronisingly and say, 'If you think he's good, you should have seen Tommy McInally.'

Yet diligent research by the young fan would show that Tommy McInally was not really all that good, or at least that he did not achieve nearly as much as he should have, if he was as talented as they all said that he was. He played only twice for Scotland, and never against England. He won the Scottish League Championship in 1922 and 1926, and in the latter part of 1922 he had dropped out of the scene, whether from genuine injury or (more likely) a fall from grace. Only once did he win the Scottish Cup, and that was in a final against a Second Division side in East Fife. He had his moments in the Glasgow Cup and the Glasgow Charity Cup (very prestigious tournaments in the 1920s) but his sojourns at other teams (Third Lanark and Sunderland) were distinct failures.

He must also take his share of blame for the general decline of Celtic in the 1920s. In the first twenty years of the twentieth century, Celtic had won the Scottish League eleven times. In the twenty years between the wars, Celtic were triumphant on only four occasions – and indeed would not regain supremacy on a permanent basis until Jock Stein arrived in 1965. In particular, McInally must shoulder a portion of the blame for the disastrous events of 1928 when a league and cup double were thrown away in the direction of Ibrox, thereby hastening his own premature departure from the team that he loved.

So why was this man, vilified and glorified in almost equal proportion by those who saw him in the 1920s, talked about so reverentially in the early 1960s? His appearances for Celtic numbered 238 and he scored 143 goals (that is according to one source – others differ – and includes the then very important Glasgow Cups and Glasgow Charity Cups). That is a fair record but other less well-known Celtic players have achieved more.

What must be recognised however is that Tommy has to be seen in the context of the times in which he lived. The 1920s are sometimes called the 'roaring twenties', and the image is conjured up of the Charleston, flappers, Agatha Christie, Percy Fender, Bertie Wooster, cinema, radio, Rudolf Valentino . . .

That is all true, but there was the other side as well. The Great War had certainly changed many things, but few were for the better. Those who survived the war often questioned who had won it. Was it, as they said, a war fought to make 'the world a safer place for Henry Ford and Pierpont Morgan', the two arch-capitalists of the day? Certainly the working man and his family did not win – they were poorer than ever, and so many households now lacked male leadership. In a way, one could say that the position of women had been strengthened – by 1928, they all had the vote – but at a terrible cost. A woman now had some power in her own house but very often only because there was no man around. And Germany, conquered and humiliated in 1919, would not go away. She was suffering worse and the world would very soon see the symptoms.

Poverty remained a vicious cancer on the soul of the population, cynically ignored by 'society' which tried to pretend that there was no such thing. The Liberal governments from 1906 until 1914 had tried to bring about some improvement, but they were being overtaken by the Labour Party as the conscience of the people. There would be minority Labour governments in 1924 and 1929–31, but it would be another twenty years before they could achieve actual control. In the meantime, unemployment, slums, appalling health conditions and an educational system which often seemed a deliberate attempt to prevent the emergence of bright working-class children, prevailed.

Labour unrest was seen in Glasgow in 1919 and in all of Britain throughout the early 1920s, particularly in 1926 when the upper class feared its comeuppance, as had happened less than a decade earlier in Russia in 1917. Across the Irish Sea, a new nation was being born and the pangs of parturition were long and grievous. That particular problem was of course of tremendous relevance and interest to the supporters of Celtic Football Club but many people remained vindictive towards the Germans, an attitude which perhaps encouraged the Germans to wage war once more – and soon.

But Glasgow also retained its humour, its decency and its love of football as crowds flocked to the games. The crowds included those who could not afford the money to get in but hung around outside while the game was in progress listening to the roars of the crowd and arguing about the game – until with 15 minutes to go, the exit gates were opened to allow the crowd *out* – and this mini-army of the poverty stricken *in* to see heroes like Alan Morton, Andrew Wilson, Tommy Cairns, Hughie Gallacher, Patsy Gallacher and Tommy McInally. But who was Tommy McInally?

His forebears undeniably came from Ireland. The name alone would tell one that. Professor Edward MacLysaght, an acknowledged expert in Irish names, tells us that the name was prevalent in Oriel (Armagh, Monaghan, Fermanagh, Down and Louth). There are several variants like McNally, McAnnally and even perhaps Lally and McNulty, but the name McInally is an anglicised form of the Gaelic 'Mac an Fhailghigh' meaning 'son of the poor man'. Although the name is particularly common in Armagh and Monaghan in

Ulster (it also occurs, albeit more rarely, in Leinster and Connaught), the explanation that it is really 'Mac Con Uladh', which means 'son of the hound of Ulster', is possible, but less likely.

As far as Tommy is concerned, there is immediately a problem, for we know very little about his early days, other than that he was brought up in Barrhead – or the surrounding area. But who was he? Four Thomas McInallys were born around 1900 in that area, but none of them absolutely fits the bill. So we look for his death certificate, which might give us an indication of when and where he was born. The newspapers tell us that he died on 29 December 1955 at the age of 'about fifty-five' and 'in a Glasgow hospital'. But no Thomas McInally died on that day in Scotland, although there was one who died in September of that year, and historians have tended to assume that this was the great Tommy McInally of Celtic.

The newspapers are not likely to be wrong on the subject of the date on which he died, although vague phrases like 'in a Glasgow hospital' are hardly historical evidence, and in this case, wrong. But if no Tommy or Thomas McInally died on that day, it follows that his real name cannot have been Thomas McInally. Was he born as Thomas something else, then adopted by a kindly Mrs McInally? This was certainly the interpretation of the very fine *Alphabet of the Celts*, written by Eugene MacBride, Martin O'Connor and George Sheridan in 1994. He had a brother called Arthur who also played professional football, but were they brothers in the strict biological sense of the word? The evidence seemed to make that unlikely. And when and where was

5

Arthur born? Again there were several possibilities, but no definitive proof of the birth of an Arthur McInally who had a brother called Tom, Tommy or Thomas.

But then, a further search of the records revealed that a *Bernard* McInally died on 29 December 1955. He was aged fifty-six and his death certificate was signed by his brother Arthur. Bernard was a commercial traveller, unmarried and had been suffering from carcinoma of the fauces (throat cancer) for two years. He lived at Crinan, 111 Paisley Road, Barrhead and died there at 3.15am. He was the son of Francis McInally and Annie Slaven. Is this our man?

We then look for Bernard's birth, and find that he was born on 18 December 1899 at 248 Main Street, Barrhead, the son of Francis McInally (an illiterate carter) and Annie Slaven who had been married in 1877. These two also had a son called Arthur born on 25 January 1895. In total there was a family of nine, five boys and four girls and Bernard was the youngest. The others were James, Francis, John, Sara, Roseanne, Ellen, Mary and Arthur.

This does indeed look like our man, but there are still anomalies. One was that he must have been a very late baby if he was born twenty-two years after his parents were married, and the unanswered question remains, why, if he was called Bernard, did he choose to call himself Tommy? It is of course by no means unheard of (nor is it in any way illegal) for someone to choose another name for himself if he does not like the one he was given, but it still seems odd that the famous name 'Tommy McInally', much repeated and sung about in the 1920s, is in fact technically wrong.

But it is clear that from an early stage, he was known as Thomas. As early as Hogmanay 1899, for example, when according to the Baptismal Register of St. John's R.C. Church, Barrhead, Father Bernard Tracy baptised one Thomas Bernard McInally. (Curiously, for reasons as yet unexplained, at a later date, someone has put a thin line through the 'Thomas' and written 'John' above!) Then in the Census Records of 1901, a 'Thomas McInally aged one' is mentioned at the appropriate address.

Bernard's (or Thomas's) father Francis was illiterate at the time of his marriage in 1877. This is no slur, because at that time quite a few working men were illiterate. Scotland prided itself (not without cause) on having the best education system in the world but to our modern eyes it was grossly inadequate. It was only in 1872 that the Scottish Education Act came into force, compelling every local authority to provide education. Prior to that, the only education had come from the Church – the Presbyterian Church – and for Roman Catholic families any education at all would have been on a haphazard and fitful basis.

Francis McInally was not one of the many who fled Ireland in the immediate aftermath of the Famine of the late 1840s. The likelihood is that he came over to Scotland as a young man in the 1870s (he does not appear in the Census of 1871) as part of the general diaspora of Irish people looking for work in the ever expanding British Industrial Revolution which had now been going strong for fifty years and more. We cannot say exactly when Francis was born (although he was almost certainly not born in Scotland) but he was the son of Rose Connelly and Bernard McInally, and we know that his father Bernard died before 1877.

Thus young Bernard may have been named after his grandfather, or even the priest, Father Bernard Tracy, who baptised him. Francis McInally died at 248 Main Street, Barrhead on 6 February 1903 of acute pulmonary congestion which he had had for ten days. Curiously, the death certificate says that he was forty-three – something that is unlikely and is at odds with his Marriage Certificate of 1877 which says he was twenty-four. Francis certainly died young but fifty would seem to be a more likely age. Having had various jobs with horses, not surprising for someone whose roots were agricultural, his last job was as a general labourer with the Gas Works.

His wife Annie, Tommy's mother, lived on until 1939, by which time she was eighty-five. She would therefore have been around to see Tommy (or Bernard's) footballing career. She was clearly a strong character and had quite an effect on her family. Annie Slaven was Scottish, although of Irish descent, as her name (and that of her mother Sara Donnelly) might indicate. She was born around 1854 in Barrhead and was the daughter of a quarrier. She worked in the cotton mills for a while but at the time that she met and married Francis McInally she was working on a farm near Nitshill.

But the young Bernard, presumably called Bernie or Barney but whom history now calls Tommy, was only three years old when his father died. This explains much of Tommy's character, for he clearly lacked a father figure in his life, although his elder brothers had quite an influence on him. Willie Maley, the Celtic manager, obviously saw himself in the 'father' role. Maley, a man whose domestic circumstances had been far from happy, quite often fancied himself as a father substitute. He blatantly tried to become Jimmy McGrory's substitute father when Henry McGrory died in a freak accident in 1924, and there is little doubt that he felt he could do a similar job with Tommy McInally. With Tommy, however, he was somewhat less successful.

Not a great deal is known of Tommy's early life but we can hazard a guess that he modelled himself on his older brother Arthur, who became a footballer as well. Like Arthur and another older brother John, who played for the now defunct Paisley side Abercorn, Tommy started off as a centre half. They were built for it. John, Arthur and James, yet another older brother, formed part of a tug-of-war team which took part in local fairs. Whilst his brothers were all over six feet in height, Tommy was of a slighter figure and, although taller than the average man in the 1920s, was a few inches short of six feet. It was soon discovered that centre half was not his position.

Quite a few people insisted that Arthur was a better player than Tommy but Arthur clearly decided, after a few years of football, that he wanted to be a teacher – a far more reliable job than a professional footballer – and taught for several years at St. Mary's School, Greenock and also at another school called St. Serf's. He married, had children and died in 1966. He was an interesting character in his own right. Arthur's footballing career was far more peripatetic than Tommy's, for after his one and only game for Celtic against Motherwell in a 4–3 win at Fir Park on 15 December 1917, he moved on to play as a part-timer for St. Mirren, Abercorn, Dunfermline Athletic, Armadale, Alloa and St. Bernard's (as well as many spells on loan to other clubs) before he became a Division Two referee in 1929 and then secretary/manager of St. Anthony's in 1935.

Arthur's one game for the club tells us a great deal of the chaotic situation that prevailed in the difficult years of the War. On 15 December 1917, Alec McNair was due to play at right back, but couldn't get a train from Stenhousemuir to Motherwell as transport had been so disrupted. The game was delayed ten minutes, but still no Alec. It being December, the game had to start to guarantee a finish in daylight. After ten minutes' play, Maley decided to give up on any chance of McNair arriving, moved right half Jimmy Wilson back to right back, then put Arthur McInally, nominally a centre half, into the right half position. By all accounts, Arthur played well, as Celtic won a tight game 4–3.

Life would have been tough for Annie McInally bringing up a family on her own after 1903. She would hardly have been the only widow around, for these were hard times, but in Annie's case she was no longer young. If we can believe her marriage certificate, she was twenty-two in 1877 so was forty-four or forty-five when Tommy was born – making Tommy a very late baby indeed. But this also means that most of her older children would have been self-supporting for a large part of Tommy's childhood. Only Tommy, Arthur and Mary would have been dependent on her. Although some of the older offspring would still have been living in the house, they were of an age to be earning for themselves. Annie also had the great advantage of a certain amount of money. She was not poor. When her husband died the extended family came to the rescue, as was expected in those days, and her brothers, the Slavens, being businessmen in the housing trade, would give Annie sufficient money to get by – and more. She was able to send young Tommy to St. Aloysius.

He had started at St. John's Primary in Barrhead. This school was built in 1906 (the Edwardian era was a great time for building schools) to replace a pre-existing building which had been there since the 1840s and Tommy would have been one of the first intake at the new building if, as he claims himself in his memoirs, he went to school when he was six. He also claims that he passed the 'qualie' (qualifying) exam at the age of ten. Whether that is true or not, he certainly went to St. Aloysius in 1912 and went straight into second year. He was clearly a bright pupil and did well at school.

St. Mungo's Academy also claims Tommy and Arthur as former pupils. This school was founded in the Garngad area of Glasgow in 1858 with the laudable object of providing education for poor Catholic boys. The school claimed to have pupils from as far away as Stirlingshire and Ayrshire, given the lack of Catholic secondary schools in these areas. Tommy went there sometime during the Great War and it was with these schools that he played organised football for the first time, being at this stage a centre half.

He claims that a harsh refereeing decision finished him with schools football. One day when playing for St. Mungo's v Dumbarton Higher Grade School, he found himself, as centre half, against a boy called J. B. Bell who would in later years play for Queen's Park. Bell was faster than Tommy and Tommy's only way of stopping him was to trip him up. Tommy was promptly sent off and suspended for a year. A year's suspension seems tough and even draconian, but schools football was like that in those days. There is also the suspicion that Tommy was perhaps being economical with the truth in his memoirs (a school jotter containing about twenty pages) and there may have been a lot more to the incident than that. Whatever happened, Tommy never played schools football again.

It was during this suspension that he went to Clydebank one day, without the knowledge of his mother, to meet John Logan of Croy Celtic. Tommy had heard that Croy Celtic, who were playing an away game there against Yoker Athletic, were interested in him. But Mr Logan did not fancy Tommy as a centre half, for he was too light and thin. Tommy, cheeky and confident, as always, nevertheless offered to play in some other position. Logan thought he would be a better forward and gave him a few games for the Croy Celtic team (the war was still going on and the manpower shortage meant that it was not too difficult to get a game of football) at inside right or centre forward.

In one of his early games Tommy was involved in a 'Hand of God' Maradona-type incident. Croy Celtic were a goal down late in the game and a high ball came across from the right wing just too high for Tommy who then handled the ball into the net and, as the referee was far away, the goal was given. The team reached the final of the Dunbartonshire Cup of 1918 but lost 0–4 in a replayed final after a draw where Tommy regretted not having taken a fairly straightforward chance when he shot straight at the goalkeeper instead of angling the ball past him. Tommy said that very soon he earned the very flattering nickname of 'Quinn' after the great Jimmy Quinn of Celtic, Croy's greatest son and Tommy's hero, who had only just recently hung up his boots.

Tommy had only been fourteen when the Great War started, just too young to have been part of the passionate but misguided march to slaughter in answer to the pointing finger of Lord Kitchener and 'your country needs you'. He was spared serving in the Great War but it would have been interesting to see how Tommy would have coped with the strict army discipline. Would he have reacted better to Maley's strict discipline in later years in civvy street? Or, more likely perhaps, would he have been even more cussed and awkward after his demob? All this of course pre-supposes that he would have survived the slaughter. So many didn't.

Football was one of the main antidotes to the horrible things that were happening in Europe. Tommy played the game for the Croy Celtic team and it soon became obvious that he had talent. Towards the end of the Great War, just as the 1918/19 season was starting, Tommy joined the famous St. Anthony's team – the Ants – taking full advantage of the shortage of manpower to earn his place. Little is known of his career for the Ants, for junior matches are not well reported in newspapers in the time of the Great War, but Tommy himself talked highly of his experiences and expressed admiration for an unlikely sort of person – a referee!

This was one Jamie Dixon who had served in India and handled junior games well, seldom having to send anyone off, for his caustic humour and rapier repartee were usually sufficient to defuse difficult situations.

St. Anthony's were a Govan-based club who played at a ground called Moore Park. Among their other 'graduates' they list Jimmy 'Sniper' McColl, Tommy's immediate predecessor as Celtic centre forward and a man who played a glorious part in Celtic's 1913/14 double winning season, not to mention the four-in-a-row League Championship successes from 1914 to 1917. They claim to have worn the green and white hoops from their foundation in 1902, but the claim that Celtic deliberately copied them in 1903 in their choice of strip is open to question. In 1918 St. Anthony's were a prestigious Glasgow outfit and Tommy, advised by brother Arthur, thought it would be a good idea to join them.

Tommy must have played well for the Ants in season 1918/19 for he attracted the attention of several big English clubs, notably Bury and Manchester City. Ernest Magnall, the manager of Manchester City, offered Tommy a huge salary to move down to England, but Tommy, very fond of Glasgow, was loath to leave his family and particularly his widowed mother who doted on her youngest son. Magnall would try again in a couple of years' time, and would get a similar answer.

Closer to home, however, was William Wilton of Rangers. St. Anthony's played virtually in the shadow of Ibrox and it was only natural that Rangers looked there first. Tommy had a couple of trials for Rangers during the 1918/19 season but his Ibrox career never really started. There is no official record of him having played a real game for Rangers so the trials would have been 'closed door' affairs. Later, on at least one occasion, Rangers renewed their interest in Tommy, but at this point, for one reason or another, nothing really happened. Perhaps he played badly in his trials, perhaps his style of play did not suit Rangers, perhaps he did or said something that blotted his copybook, but one factor I think can be discounted.

That is the one of religion. Later in the 1920s at Ibrox, a stern 'No Catholics' policy developed under Bill Struth, but in 1918/19, although there was a tendency for players at Ibrox to be of the Protestant faith because most Irish Catholics tended to aspire to play for Celtic, there was no hard-and-fast rule. A fair amount of Roman Catholics, notably Willie Kivlichan for example, a member of the Third Order of St. Francis, played for Rangers without any apparent harassment. Tommy McInally, if good enough, would have been made welcome at Ibrox at that time. Religion might have been an issue in 1925 when feelers were put out to Tommy by some unofficial Ibrox sources (it was said), and it certainly would have been an issue from the 1930s until the late 1980s, but in 1919, probably not.

But there was little doubt who Tommy wanted to play for most of all. People of Irish descent gravitated towards the great organisation which allowed the Irish in Glasgow to feel good about themselves, the Celtic team, founded for the purpose of feeding poor Catholic children and which had played its first game in 1888. In his infancy and early childhood, Tommy would have heard about the great team that won six League Championships in a row, about Young, Loney and Hay, about the great Jimmy Quinn and Jimmy McMenemy. Perhaps one of his elder brothers or a neighbour might have taken him to see them. In his teens it was Patsy Gallacher who was 'the most talked about man in the trenches, on the High Seas and in faraway Mesopotamia' and there would have been no doubt that if it came to a choice between Celtic and any other team there would have been little hesitation on the part of young Tommy McInally.

He was nineteen years old when the call came.

2

The Dream Debutant 1919/20

One often shudders to think what the West of Scotland would have been like without Celtic. Since their inception some thirty years previously, they had been phenomenally successful with great players and the ability to pick up trophies. This success had been the rallying point for the Irish community in Glasgow and although there was a reaction of dislike for them in certain quarters, the team had done a great deal to embed the Irish in the Scottish community. Without a great team to support, the Irish might well have turned to less peaceful pursuits. Particularly in the Great War, the wholehearted support given by the Irish community might have been less forthcoming, and there would have been a danger of the sizeable Glasgow Irish community becoming a disillusioned sub-culture in the way that certain sections of the Islamic community can be perceived today. Is it too fanciful to imagine, for example, that the Easter Rising in Dublin in 1916 might well have been replicated, or certainly strongly supported in Glasgow?

No less important a point in the rise of the club had

been the spreading of the tradition of good football. McMahon, Doyle, Young, Loney, Hay, McMenemy, Quinn and others had shown Scotland how the game should be played, and the name Celtic had gained a great deal of affection and support from areas other than the immediate catchment area of the Glasgow Irish. Support in the North, East and South of Scotland for the 'bould Celts', 'mighty Celts' and the 'Tim Malloys' among the non-Catholic section of the community was an eloquent tribute to Willie Maley's footballing brain and the broad-based selection policy which, even from the early days, would include non-Catholics. 'It is not his creed or his nationality that counts, it's the man himself,' is self-evident today. It was less so a hundred years ago and Maley must be given credit for his foresight.

The character of Willie Maley (rightly called 'The Man Who Made Celtic') had been crucial to the rise of Celtic and would continue to be crucial to the future development of the club, not least in regards to how Tommy McInally would react to the demands of professional football. Maley was technically an Irishman, born in Newry, the son of a British soldier. A fine athlete, cyclist and football player, he had joined Celtic in 1888 and indeed played in their very first game, then won a Scottish Cup medal in 1892 and Scottish League medals in 1893 and 1894. By far the proudest moments of his playing career however were the two 'caps' that he won for Scotland, a very potent symbol of how he, an Irishman, had been accepted by the Scottish establishment.

In the aftermath of Celtic's disastrous Scottish Cup

defeat in 1897 at Arthurlie, by sheer coincidence, about half a mile from where Tommy McInally would be born two years later, Maley was appointed Celtic's first secretary/manager. He remained totally devoted to the club for the next sixty years of his life, even after he was sacked in 1940, and for Maley the idea of acceptability by Scottish society was always an important factor. He did not want Celtic to lapse back into some persecuted, ghetto-mentality, introverted organisation and he wanted Celtic players to be a credit to themselves, the club and the game.

He was a great motivator of players and knew what a good player was. His and Celtic's record from 1904 until 1910 spoke for itself. But the success had not been achieved without a price. Maley's marriage had failed and he had the reputation of being, on occasion, a brooding, difficult-to-live-with man. He was a natural dictator and did not brook much opposition to his ideas. He was strict, at least on the outside, but that was only half the story, for he was cheerful, genial and outgoing as well with a perpetual desire to talk about football and his beloved Celtic. Like a few dictators, there was a 'soft' side to Maley too. Like Stein a generation or two later, he knew the benefit of good public relations.

Celtic had prospered during the Great War. Beginning from the base of being League and Cup double winners in 1914, they had won the Scottish League in 1915, 1916, 1917 and 1919, only narrowly missing out to Rangers in 1918. The Scottish Cup was not competed for during the war but the Glasgow Cup had been won twice and the Charity Cup four times.

Contrary to what many people have thought subsequently, football was taken very seriously indeed during the war and news of Celtic's successes was greeted with great joy among their supporters in the various theatres of war and on the home front.

The unkind had called Celtic the 'war profiteers' for their financial position was robust. A large part of this was due to the financial management of Willie Maley and his almost uncanny ability to keep most of his good players out of the forces, though not all of them. Peter Johnstone, the great half back, had heeded the call to arms and had perished in 1917, but most of Maley's fine side had avoided the conflict. Any sneers of 'war dodging' could easily be answered by Maley pointing to the excellent job that his men had done in the munitions industries and the entertainment that Celtic had provided for soldiers on leave and for those with heavy hearts on the home front. In any case, men like Joe Cassidy, Willie McStay and Andy McAtee had all served and many supporters had perished at the front.

The armistice had been signed on 11 November 1918 but the war did not technically come to an end until the following summer. Season 1918/19 had been a wartime season with no Scottish Cup and no Internationals, other than the unofficial Victory games, but Celtic did regain the Scottish League championship at Ayr on 10 May 1919. The league business over, centre forward Jimmy 'Sniper' McColl, who had been struggling for some time with a bad leg, gave notice that he was going to hospital in the summer for an operation.

It would be no easy task to replace the prolific 'Sniper' but Maley had had his eye on St. Anthony's

Tommy McInally who, Maley was well aware, had also been given a trial for Rangers. Maley invited the tall, slim youngster to join Celtic for a friendly to be played on the island of Bute, at Rothesay Public Park against a Bute Select on 17 May 1919. Celtic cultivated good relationships with the people of Bute and Maley, as always, very keen on the 'missionary' aspect of Celtic, was careful to ensure that the 2,000-strong crowd would see some of the more established Celtic players as well as some juniors. Charlie Shaw, Andy McAtee and Joe Cassidy all played that day but trialist McInally stole the show, scoring in the thirtieth minute and then twice in the second half as Celtic romped home 6–0.

This was a friendly game but the following week's game was not. McInally was not in the side which lost 3–1 to Queen's Park, the first time that the Spiders had beaten Celtic since 1903, in the Glasgow Charity Cup semi final and this dismal performance convinced Maley that McInally should be officially signed from St. Anthony's for Celtic by the start of next season, the first official season after the Great War.

St. Anthony's (the Ants) were a curious side but a very successful nursery of talent. They played within sight of Ibrox but with their green and white jerseys they kept their feet in both camps, as it were. Maley however took not only McInally from the Ants in 1919 but Johnny McKay and Johnny Gilchrist too. McKay would be less successful than the other two but Gilchrist would form part of the mighty Gilchrist, Cringan and McMaster half back line of the early 1920s. Like McInally, Gilchrist would find the iron discipline of Maley hard to handle.

Thus the young McInally was now a professional football player. It is hard to imagine or recreate the excitement of that 1919 summer as the football season approached. The soldiers were all coming back home, apart from those who were still involved in the foolish Civil War in Russia and, closer to home and to the hearts of Celtic fans, in the complicated strife in Ireland. Sinn Féin, having won seventy-five out of 105 seats in the December 1918 election, saw the result as a mandate to set up their own parliament, the Dáil in Dublin – but the British government would not give in gracefully. Troops were deployed there 'to keep the peace' and very soon the following year they were supplemented by the brutalised ex-servicemen and the convicted criminals who would be called the Black and Tans.

Even closer to home was the business in Glasgow at the end of January 1919 when Lloyd George's panicky coalition government were so afraid of Bolshevik revolution that troops had to be deployed to be kept in readiness in case demonstrations in George Square got out of control. They were not actually used (and the troops stationed at Maryhill barracks were so close to mutiny and to actually joining the protesters that they had to be confined there!) because the police were brutal enough at dispersing the protesters but the very fact that the military was there added an extra dimension to the labour disputes that were going on in the aftermath of the Great War.

Both these stories in Glasgow and Ireland had a great deal to run and affected intimately Celtic and their supporters but, on the other hand, excitement was definitely in the air. Everyone was happy just to be alive and the new football season seemed to be almost a catharsis for all the terrible things that happened in the war. The pain would not of course go away and there were far too many disabled men, wretched widows and fatherless bairns around to allow anyone to forget, but football at least was back. Some kind of normality was restored.

The Scottish League realised this enthusiasm for the new season and raised prices from 8d to one shilling, five pence in modern reckoning. While this was clothed in terminology like 'rising costs', it was seen as little other than an attempt to exploit the obvious passion for the game. There was the undeniable fact that, for all the suffering that the war had brought, there was more money around. Many men had come home from the war with more money in their pocket than they would normally have. 'Severance pay' and 'demobilisation allowance' meant that there was, temporarily at least, more money in circulation than there would be a few years later. In addition, those who had worked in the munitions industries had been well rewarded for their efforts. Football was trying to get its share.

An attempt was made by a few fans, spearheaded by some politicians of the Socialist and Labour Parties which had already made a great impact on post-war Scotland, to boycott the games of the new season until such time as the authorities recanted but the idea never took off. Politics was one thing, football was something sacred! The rise, although steep, was affordable by most fans and in any case the full charge of one shilling was paid by comparatively few of the crowd for there was a boys' gate (and quite a few mature looking 'boys' queued up for that one!), a disabled gate, a veterans gate or an unemployed gate at most grounds, particularly at Parkhead where Maley won much admiration for his desire to 'help the lame dog over the stile' and to encourage as large a crowd as possible.

In the event 12,000, a respectable but not huge attendance for the time, turned up at Celtic Park to see the league champions take on Clydebank on 16 August 1919. A stirring sight was witnessed as the war blinded and other disabled men in 'hospital blue' uniform, some in wheelchairs, were ushered into the game, the blind to hear a commentary on the game from a stentorian-voiced volunteer. It would be from this genesis that the idea of broadcasting a game on the radio would develop a few years later.

At full time both the disabled and the able-bodied talked about little other than Tommy McInally, who scored a hat-trick in Celtic's 3–1 defeat of the visitors. *The Glasgow Observer* dubbed him 'the apostle of direct action' for his first time shooting. *The Glasgow Herald* was similarly impressed:

> The Celts appear to have secured in McInally a worthy successor to Quinn. To score three goals on a first appearance is certainly promising as no other Celtic forward got the better of McTurk whose saving of other splendid shots from McInally was the feature of the Clydebank defence.

McInally scored early on, then Clydebank equalised almost immediately before McInally scored with Celtic's first attack of the second half and then finished the job against a tired Clydebank defence. The team was Shaw, McNair and Livingstone, McStay, Cringan and Brown, Watson, Gallacher, McInally, McMenemy and McLean.

The phrase 'dream debut' hardly does credit to this performance. Already compared with Jimmy Quinn! Here was a young lad in his first game playing alongside men like Charlie Shaw, Eck McNair, Patsy Gallacher and Jimmy McMenemy – household names in Scotland and throughout the world – and scoring a hat-trick! Of course playing between two inside men of the calibre of Patsy Gallacher and Jimmy McMenemy, the cynics would have said that anyone could score goals.

To an extent this was true – Patsy Gallacher, 'the most talked about man in the trenches', was already a legend for his wizardly dribbles and Jimmy 'Napoleon' McMenemy who had been around now for the best part of twenty years (and twenty glorious years at that!) had shrugged off illness in the shape of Spanish flu and confounded all those stories about him being 'finished' (he would yet win more caps for Scotland and win a Scottish Cup winner's medal in 1921, albeit not with Celtic) to earn compliments like 'the most accomplished player in the Scottish footballing world'.

Young Tommy had barely time to draw breath or to bask in his achievement before he was in action again. Two days later, on a Monday evening, Dumbarton came to Parkhead and shocked the 8,000-strong crowd by going ahead before McInally equalised before half time ('a hooked shot from close quarter'), put Celtic in the lead in the seventy-eighth minute and then as time ran out slipped the ball to McMenemy to put Celtic 3–1 up. Some sources give this goal to McInally himself, but even if it was Napoleon who applied the finishing touch, this still made five goals in two games – enough to draw attention to the fact that Celtic had a real player here.

Such is the ethos of this great club that a personality goalscorer is a 'sine qua non'. Already Celtic had had three great centre forwards in Sandy McMahon, Jimmy Quinn and Jimmy McColl. Optimists now began to think that Tommy McInally might eclipse them all. Sadly and tragically, perhaps Tommy McInally himself, ever ready to bask in adulation, began to get the idea that he might be the greatest of them all.

But for the moment, Tommy and the team continued to prosper. August ended with Celtic retaining their 100 per cent record and the exciting inside right trio of Gallacher, McInally and McMenemy looking virtually unbeatable. Goals kept coming for Tommy – one at Douglas Park, Hamilton and two against Raith Rovers at Parkhead. His first goal against Raith Rovers was a 'reward for craft'. He found himself sandwiched between two burly Raith defenders as he ran in on goal. A player like Jimmy Quinn would have used his shoulders to barge them out of the way but Tommy, realising wisely that he was too slight for this, turned and drove the ball out to Andy McAtee on the wing. Then he niftily dodged the two defenders, allowed them to crash into each other while he positioned himself perfectly for Andy's return cross, rose like a bird to connect with it and gave goalkeeper Clark 'not an earthly'.

The first concrete success for Tommy came in the Glasgow Cup. This tournament was taken very seriously in those days and was played for by the six teams of Glasgow – Celtic, Rangers, Partick Thistle, Queen's

Park, Third Lanark and Clyde. In the first round there were two ties and two byes, then a straight knock-out semi final and final, normally played on the October holiday weekend. Winning the Glasgow Cup was always a great feeling for supporters in that they could face what the winter was to throw at them secure in the knowledge that at least one trophy was in the bag.

It was also a tournament that was allowed to take precedence over Scottish League games. It was older than the Scottish League and the view was taken that cup games were more important than league ones. League games could always be played later. This idea of allowing a local tournament to push national ones out of the way was resented by provincial teams, but then as now, money and population were very important factors.

As luck would have it, Celtic were drawn at home against Rangers in the first round on 6 September 1919. The fixture attracted 63,000, by some distance the biggest ever attendance yet for a Glasgow Cup match and beaten only once or twice before the war in Scottish Cup finals. Such was the madness and passion which associated itself with Scottish football in 1919. It was Adam McLean who scored the only goal of the game but it had been set up by some fine play from McInally, who was described as a 'tireless forager'. Rangers claimed hard luck, but they did not help their cause when Jimmy Walls was sent off for kicking Patsy Gallacher.

Then a couple of weeks later in the semi final, the 'boy wonder', as he was now called, scored a hat-trick as Queen's Park were put to the sword by a rampant Celtic team in the eccentric strip of green shirts with a white diamond (in the style of the white and red of Airdrieonians). The first was described as a 'great shot', the second was a rebound off the bar following a Joe Cassidy shot and the third was a great header from a cross from Andy McAtee.

The Glasgow Herald was more impressed by the behaviour of both teams:

> Seldom can a cup tie be held up as an object lesson in deportment and probably no other teams could have taken a semi final tie in the same keen yet friendly spirit as the representatives of clubs as mutually respected as Queen's Park and Celtic.

So as yet there was no dent in the halo of Tommy McInally and his stock rose even further in a league game the following week against Clyde when Celtic were 0–1 down with seventeen minutes to go but won 3–1 and Tommy scored all three goals! They were described as a 'long fast drive', a 'penalty rebound' and a 'placed shot'. The week after that he scored two against Third Lanark. Was there any stopping the 'boy wonder'?

Fourth October 1919 saw all of Great Britain in the throes of a railway strike with the railwaymen asking Lloyd George in newspaper adverts: 'What happened to the land fit for heroes to live in?'. In spite of obvious transport difficulties, 45,000 were at Parkhead to see Celtic win the Glasgow Cup by beating Partick Thistle 1–0. Some sources say that it was Adam McLean who scored the only goal of the game but *The Glasgow Herald* is emphatic that it was McInally who scored that day with 'an overhead shot which surprised the goal-keeper and probably himself'. This is damning with faint praise and one gets the impression that the writer has Partick Thistle sympathies as he emphasises that it was a 'featureless final'.

A more positive account of McInally's goal comes from *The Glasgow Observer*, an avowedly pro-Celtic newspaper. It tells us that Partick Thistle's left back Bullock cleared a ball and while the ball was still in the air, McInally hit it first time and with a delicate lob completely deceived Stewart in the goal. This is either a fluke or genius, according to your perspective. The Celtic fans went for genius. McInally's play was outstanding throughout the ninety minutes (in spite of a few curmudgeonly remarks from *The Glasgow Herald*) and less than two months after making his debut, Tommy McInally had already scored sixteen goals, won a Glasgow Cup medal and earned a place in the hearts of the Celtic faithful.

The teams were:

Celtic: Shaw, McNair and McStay; Gilchrist, Cringan and Cassidy; McAtee, Gallacher, McInally, McMenemy and McLean.

Partick Thistle: Stewart, Adams and Bullock; Black, Hamilton and McMullan; McLachlan, Lauder, Harris, Mitchell and Bowie.

Celtic fans could hardly believe they were alive. They had now won the Glasgow Cup twelve times in little more than thirty years of existence and it seemed that the team was simply picking up where they left off before the War. No trains of course that day, so the supporters made their way back to their homes on foot (some of them, the war wounded, with extreme difficulty) singing the praises of the 'boy wonder' and looking forward to buying at least one of Glasgow's three evening papers, the *News*, the *Citizen* or the *Times*, to revel in this great day.

Such a crazy whirlwind start could not last, for Tommy was still just a young lad as yet without the maturity to pace himself and, worse still, without the ability to resist the blandishments and adulation of his loving fans. In a remarkable game at Parkhead, Celtic beat Hibs 7–3 with McInally scoring twice but then Rangers hit back at Celtic in mid-October by winning 3–0 at Ibrox in a game where Tommy was barely mentioned in reports of the game, so well contained were the Celtic inside trio by Rangers' half back line of Bowie, Dixon and Walls. Reports of this game also talk about the crowd – a massive gathering of 70,000 – and songs being sung by ex-servicemen wearing captured German helmets painted green and white or blue according to the persuasion of their owner!

For the rest of 1919, Tommy's form now tailed off. Sometimes he was rested and replaced by Jimmy McColl (now recovered from his operation) and goals certainly dried up, both for Celtic and for McInally himself as conditions deteriorated. November 1919 was one of the coldest months on record in Scotland with temperatures at times dipping to minus fifteen at Balmoral and even to minus twenty-two at Braemar and McInally's trickery was a great deal less effective in the fog and ice of November and the heavy, muddy pitches of December. The year turned with Celtic, in spite of their bright start, behind Rangers in the league.

Maley was not at this stage overly worried for he knew that in McInally he had someone who could win him games. He was careful, however, how he played him. McInally was young, fit, athletic and fast. It would have been a great temptation for Maley to overload him, for the youngster was enthusiastic and trained hard. Maley felt, however, that he understood the youngster and that he had to be husbanded carefully. But Maley was also aware that the key games were to come in the New Year.

The Roaring Twenties began with McInally leading the line in front of a huge 75,905 crowd at Parkhead on New Year's Day and playing respectably in a hard fought 1–1 draw on a frosty pitch. In fact, he might have won the game if he had first-timed a McMenemy pass instead of trying to show off by lobbing the full back and thus giving the goalkeeper time to get back. In passing we can note the boom in football at this time because in addition to the huge crowd at Parkhead, there were at least 40,000 at Hampden to see the 'all-amateur' game between Queen's Park and their English counterparts, the Corinthians.

Two days later 16,000 crammed into Stark's Park, Kirkcaldy to see a 3–0 win for Celtic and the town's citizens amazed at the amount of 'charabancs and omnibuses' (at least twenty according to some witnesses) from the west of Scotland. These new motorised vehicles had replaced the pre-war horse drawn brake clubs and had the advantage that they could travel further. Supporters could now make a day out of a trip to towns like Kirkcaldy on these buses bedecked in the team's colours and blowing bugles as they sang their team's songs. It was the custom to name the bus after a player and it was not uncommon to see 'Glasgow Tommy McInally' or 'Coatbridge Tommy McInally' chalked on the side of a vehicle.

At the end of January and the beginning of February, Celtic played at Dundee in successive weeks, one game in the league and one in the cup. Celtic kept the team in Angus at the Bruce Hotel, Carnoustie for the week between the games where the players were able to train, endear themselves to the local population by being permanently available for press interviews and photographs and play golf under the stern tutelage of Willie Maley. In later years, such trips would spell trouble for McInally but at this stage he was impeccably behaved with Maley keeping a proprietorial eye on his young protégé.

One thing that did emerge about McInally this week, though, was that he was a born entertainer both on and off the field. It was the custom for Celtic to take it upon themselves when on an away trip to entertain the other guests at the hotel with a soiree of songs, recitations and general jollity. This was of course excellent public relations and had the additional benefit that Maley could more easily keep his eye on his players. *The Dundee Courier* went out of its way to describe Maley as a 'genial host' and mentioned that several Celtic players, including the 'boy wonder' McInally, had fine voices as they performed their repertoire of Scottish and Irish songs. The song that everyone was singing at that time was

'There's a long, long trail awinding into the land of my dreams', a song made popular during the war and now drooled over by the maudlin and sentimental survivors.

> There's a long, long trail awinding
> Into the land of my dreams
> Where the nightingale sings sweetly
> And the pale moon beams.
> There's a long, long trail awinding
> Until all my dreams come true
> Until the day that I'll be walking
> Down that long, long trail with you!

McInally, in fact, had not played in the first of the Dundee games. He was injured. As a result perhaps, Celtic had lost, thus impairing their league championship challenge, but he was recalled for the Cup tie. Dundee's roads could barely cope with the volume of traffic for this game and a record crowd of 34,786 was there to see Celtic win 3–1, scoring goals at the start of each half. McInally, in the team because Jimmy McColl was ill (although Maley might have brought him back in any case), fed McLean at the start of the first half, then scored himself at the start of the second with the first 'run through' of the second half. So Celtic had lost to Dundee when McInally was out but had beaten them when McInally played! There was a lesson here which Maley did not heed.

McInally would also score in the next round of the Scottish Cup when an astonishing 70,000 saw Celtic beat Partick Thistle 2–0 at Parkhead. But then Maley made his big mistake of the season, in the eyes of the lovers of Tommy McInally, for he opted for experience for the visit to Rangers in the quarter final. Both McMenemy and Gallacher were available (they hadn't been for various reasons earlier) and Maley made the questionable decision of playing Joe Cassidy at inside left, McMenemy at inside right and Patsy Gallacher in the centre. Thus Gallacher, great player though he was and just back from injury, was being asked to play against Rangers at Ibrox in the wrong position! This meant there was no place for Tommy McInally.

It was apparently a last-minute decision, and the wrong one, for *The Evening Times* said sadly:

> Physically, the Parkhead forwards were not big enough for their job and they were not having any luck at a time when a little of that commodity goes a long way.

Patsy Gallacher missed a golden opportunity late on and Rangers won 1–0 in a poor game in which Celtic were 'worth a draw'. Indeed their fans thought that and their frustration was apparent as some of them misguidedly invaded the field near the end in an attempt to get the game stopped so that in a replay Tommy McInally could be played!

An even nastier incident arose in another game when the crowd did manage to get a game stopped against Dundee at Parkhead on Monday 26 April. Dundee had been suspected of 'lying down' to Rangers on the Saturday (they had lost 1–6 and even their own local *Dundee Courier* had expressed surprise at the lack of cohesion and commitment of their team), and with the Celtic v Dundee game poised at 1–1, some idiots invaded the field, assaulted some Dundee players and the referee and earned the club the punishment of having the ground closed. McInally had missed that game through injury, as did Patsy Gallacher, and in their absence Dundee's rugged centre half Dyken Nicol was in total command of the Celtic forward line.

This violent behaviour by their fans cost Celtic dear and may or may not have had some connection with the police in George Square breaking up a Sinn Fein demonstration earlier that afternoon, but the league had effectively been lost earlier by two draws against Motherwell and St. Mirren. Both were bad days for McInally. The Motherwell game, played at Fir Park on the day of the Scottish Cup Final (17 April) when Kilmarnock beat Albion Rovers, saw him suffer the insult of not having his name mentioned in press reports at all. And then, after scoring twice at Easter Road and seeing Celtic to an impressive victory against Hibs, he scored against St. Mirren, then was 'lamed' by a tackle by a Paisley defender which was described, like the rest of the game, as 'unnecessarily robust', as games with St. Mirren often were. The game thus ended 2–2, and Celtic's league chances had now dwindled to virtually nil even before the events involving Dundee, a game that his injury sustained against St. Mirren compelled McInally to miss.

Thus ended Tommy McInally's first league campaign. It was disappointing after such an impressive start but there was a sting in the tail for Tommy when Celtic added to their Glasgow Cup success by lifting the Glasgow Charity Cup as well. This trophy, sometimes called the Glasgow Merchants Charity Cup, was played at the end of the season, usually in May when the season had officially finished. Proceeds did indeed go to charity and players were supposed to play for nothing or to give a large share of their match fee to worthwhile causes. Whether they did so or not is a matter of some doubt but the Charity Cup was also a trophy much cherished in its time.

Rangers were the opponents in the semi final in a game played in the gloom of mourning for their manager William Wilton, who had drowned in a boating accident in the Clyde at Gourock the previous week. Rangers' hearts were not in it, and in a poor and ill-tempered game where a man from each side, Charlie Watson of Celtic and Jimmy Gordon of Rangers, was sent off, Celtic won 2–1. McInally did not score but orchestrated his line so well that Maley began to wonder whether the best position for the Barrhead boy might not be at inside right as a 'purveyor' as well as a 'predator'.

The following week, 15 May 1920, Tommy won his second medal when an injury-weakened Celtic team were still good enough to beat Queen's Park 1–0 in front of 50,000 at Hampden. Queen's Park were a good side with a particular star in Alan Morton on the left wing, a man reputed to be on the verge of a transfer to Rangers, but that day Celtic's Eck McNair got the better of him. McInally made the only goal of the game for Adam McLean. The writer of *The Evening Times* became so enthusiastic that his syntax went somewhat askew: 'McInally got off and, beating Steel, crossed from almost the goal line and McLean charged in, drove hard and the ball squirmed under the goalkeeper's body'. It was Celtic's eighth success in nine seasons in that trophy and the seventeenth in the history of the club and 'McInally's wiles' had played a large part in winning the Cup.

The teams were:

Celtic: Shaw, McNair and Livingstone; Gilchrist,
        Cringan and McStay; Watson, McKay,
        McInally, McLean and Pratt.

Queen's Park: Hunter, Steel and Young; Donaldson,
        McKenzie and Cameron; Niven,
        Kinloch, Fyfe, McAlpine and Morton.

The season finished the following week with a 2–0 win over Hearts in a friendly for the National War Memorial Fund in a game observed by the Duke and Duchess of Atholl, who would have approved of Tommy's goal. He had come far in his first season. Two medals were already his to show off to his proud mother, family and friends, particularly his brother Arthur who was now with Dunfermline Athletic. A Scottish medal would have been nice but the two Glasgow ones were enough to be going on with. Indeed, it was significant that the Scottish Cup defeat to Rangers was a game in which Tommy did not play – a point that would be emphasised by the McInally admirers and by McInally himself, one suspects. He had also been out injured in late January when the team had lost in successive weeks at Clydebank and Dundee and then again when Dundee came to Parkhead in April – and that was how the league had been lost, according to the many McInally apologists.

Whatever McInally felt about himself, however, he never became unpleasant or conceited. Bob McPhail, who would become one of Rangers' and Scotland's greatest ever players, was slightly younger than McInally. He tells of how McInally was seen around Barrhead, buying chips from Dougie's Fish Shop at the old station after having been to the pictures, talking to everyone, once ruffling the hair of Bob and asking, 'And how's young McPhail?' to the discomfort of Bob, who was nevertheless thrilled that Tommy knew his name. Tommy's instinct was to laugh and joke with everyone and he once paid McPhail's tram fare when the youngster was short.

Still only twenty and already some sort of cult hero with the Parkhead faithful as a goalscorer (thirty-six goals in all games) and a fine player with loads of trickery and panache, the personality defects that led to his downfall were not yet apparent. The summer of 1920 was passed by Celtic fans in quiet contemplation of how, with Tommy McInally on board, the team would once again come to dominate Scottish football. Alas, the reality would be somewhat different.

3

Failing to Cope

Season 1920/21 was remarkably similar to the previous season in terms of competitions won. Once again the two Glasgow trophies were won but Rangers won the Scottish League (although again Celtic gave them a good run for their money) and the Scottish Cup went that year to Partick Thistle who surprised everyone by having the old Celtic warhorse Jimmy McMenemy at the age of thirty-nine on board when they beat Rangers in the final.

By an amazing coincidence, McInally also scored thirty-six goals in all competitions in both season 1919/20 and 1920/21 but there the similarity ends. Too often in season 1920/21 McInally had looked less fit than before and although he retained his popularity and cult hero status, there were times when exasperation was heard on the terraces. It was as if there was a feeling amongst the supporters that, although McInally was good, he could be even better.

This was not the first or last time that Celtic fans have behaved like this. One can recall Jimmy Johnstone in the 1960s, Kenny Dalglish in the 1970s and Paul

McStay in the 1980s and 1990s – good players, brilliant players perhaps, all of them – being on the wrong end of the supporters' displeasure for the occasional misplaced pass or missed chance. Celtic supporters, perhaps inured to seeing the good football that has always been the trademark of the club, find it hard to accept that a player can have an off day.

Yet McInally's off days were outnumbered by his good days, and he was still treated with affection being called 'Tommy' or 'Tommy Mack'. Songs were sung in his honour, for example to the tune of Harry Lauder's 'Roamin in the Gloamin' one could hear:

Tommy McInally – he's the best man in the land
Tommy McInally – he's the pride of the ground and stand!
Even though I get the sack – I would love my Tommy Mack,
Oh, I love you, Tommy McInally.

Tommy McInally – he's the man who makes us sing
Tommy McInally – as he charges up the wing!
And when he gets the ball, you can hear the Celtic call
Tommy, Tommy, Tommy McInally.

The reference to 'getting the sack' is presumed to have something to do with the amount of games played on a Wednesday afternoon in these pre-floodlight days and the amount of supporters who were prepared to risk the ire of their employers just to cheer on Tommy McInally.

And of course the traditional song 'Sally In Our Alley' lent itself to change by the lovers of Tommy McInally.

Of all the days within the week
I dearly love but one day;
And that's the day that comes betwixt

The Friday and the Sunday.
Of, then I'm dressed in green and white,
To go and see our 'Snally
He's the greatest in the land
He's Tommy McInally!

For it's Tom, Tom, Tom,
He belongs to the Barrhead Alley,
Tommy McInally,
For when he's on the ball
You can hear the people bawl.
'Play up, Tommy McInally'
With the ball at his feet, Tommy is a treat
Tom, Tom, Tommy McInally!

There were of course many other fine players, particularly in that forward line – Patsy Gallacher, Andy McAtee, Joe Cassidy, Adam McLean – these were all the sort of forward that a manager would die for and it was no surprise that Celtic lifted the Glasgow Cup in early October 1920. McInally played well in all three games, all of them played at Parkhead. The first game was against Third Lanark in early September on a terrible day of wind and rain when, after Celtic had faced the wind in the first half and held Thirds to 0–0, McInally scored for Celtic immediately after the break with a fierce shot ('the ball whanged with its ferocity' according to *The Glasgow Herald*) to set up a 3–0 win. Two weeks later, Celtic got the better of Rangers before a crowd of 65,282 when McInally picked up a pass from Patsy Gallacher to score just before half time then passed to Adam McLean to score a second before Rangers pulled a goal back.

Then on 2 October at Celtic Park, Tommy picked up

his second Glasgow Cup medal when an Andy McAtee goal (set up by McInally) was enough to win the trophy in the final against Clyde before a crowd given as either 37,000 or 45,000, depending on which newspaper one reads. It mattered little, for however many Celtic supporters there were at the game, they were delighted with the performance of their team. It had not, in all truth, been a great game and Clyde had been handicapped with the loss with a broken ankle of their right winger Hugh Morris just before Celtic scored the only goal of the game, but the ecstatic Celtic fans – the Glasgow Glee Club as some called them – had another trophy to cheer.

The teams were:

Celtic: Shaw, McNair and McStay; Gilchrist, Cringan and Pratt; McAtee, Gallacher, McInally, Cassidy and McLean

Clyde: Shingleton, Cowan and Farrell; Rae, Forrest and Marshall; Morris, Fleming, Quinn, Duncan and Thomson.

What distinguished McInally from the rest of this star-studded forward line was his pace. Fairly tall and slim, his pace was at one point his salvation and subsequently his downfall, for it was the lack of pace that became most obvious when Tommy began in later years to put on weight. But at that time, his speed became one of the many things which delighted Celtic fans. For example, on a billboard near Parkhead, there was an advertisement for a motor car (a post-war phenomenon) at the price of £415. Not many Celtic supporters in 1920 in the East End of Glasgow were likely to be able to afford that price, but the car was a Chevrolet and it boasted that 'it was the fastest thing on wheels'. Someone had scrawled over the billboard: 'Aye, but is it as fast as Tommy McInally?'

Then on Tuesday 5 October, while Celtic were playing a friendly game against the Central League for Charlie Shaw's Benefit, McInally was given permission by Maley (who had himself been a runner thirty years previously) to go to Shawfield to take part in an Invitation 100 yards race against a few other promising sprinters and the great William Applegarth, from Guisborough in Yorkshire. Applegarth was reckoned to be Britain's fastest athlete and a winner of both a gold and a bronze medal in the 1912 Olympics in Stockholm, but was not chosen for the 1920 Games in Antwerp because he had done some professional running in the USA during the Great War. In the event, Applegarth was over generous in giving McInally ten yards of a start, and Tommy edged home. This did little to diminish the passion for Tommy among a support who craved a personality.

Celtic went on to put five goals past Queen's Park in a game where McInally did not score but was the 'constant inspiration'. He scored twice in a midweek game against Falkirk and then ninety-three charabancs were counted in Dundee in mid-October as Celtic, before a huge crowd of 32,000, beat the home side 2–1 with McInally scoring a goal with his left foot from the edge of the box which was still talked about fifty years later. That levelled the scores and then McInally, with a mazy run, beat a few defenders to feed Andy McAtee for the winner.

Tommy (and Celtic) were a great deal less fortunate when Celtic met Rangers at Parkhead in the Scottish League on 23 October 1920. Joe Cassidy had put Celtic ahead after thirty-five minutes and Celtic had looked well on top but in the first minute of the second half, McInally limped off with what looked like a pulled muscle after he had over-reached himself to meet a McLean cross. This meant trouble for Celtic and the Rangers supporters were visibly delighted to see the departure of Tommy. Rangers then went on to equalise through Tommy Cairns and then score the winner through Alan Morton – the goal that went down in song as the 'baw that Charlie Shaw never saw'.

This song tells a great deal about the times. It was to the tune of 'The Red Flag', a song much sung in those days by the Red Clydesiders, but proscribed by the police. Thus in political demonstrations, at the sight of the 'bobbies' (a great many of whom were brutalised ex-servicemen, rather than the traditionally more cuddly 'Glesca polis' variety), the words about 'workers' flags' and 'deepest red' were very soon changed to Chairlie Shaw and Alan Morton:

> Oh Chairlie Shaw, he never saw
> Whaur Alan Morton pit the baw
> He pit the baw richt in the net
> And Chairlie Shaw sat doon and gret.

Within a matter of months, other teams had someone who had put a ball past Charlie as well – Willie Hillhouse of Albion Rovers, Alec Troup of

Dundee and Tokey Duncan of Raith Rovers all apparently achieved this feat!

What is often overlooked in the amount of romance about this song is how much a compliment it was to the great Charlie. It was not very often that a ball got past Charlie, and when it did, it was worth a song. The kindly Charlie himself was said to be greatly flattered when he heard opposition supporters singing that song.

It was not only on the labour front that there was trouble brewing, though. More intimately and poignantly for Celtic and their supporters was the war in Ireland, which in autumn 1920 was entering a particularly bloody and brutal phase. The press reported murders, reprisals and arson attacks, emphasising the wickedness of the IRA while playing down the role of the murderous ex-convicts in the auxiliary force which became known as the Black and Tans. But there were some things that could not be hidden. The Lord Mayor of Cork, Terence McSweeney, died on hunger strike in Brixton Prison; a young man called Kevin Barry was hanged after torture (both of these events would become much commemorated in song) and then, to cap it all, on Sunday 21 November, the Black and Tans opened fire on a Gaelic football crowd at Croke Park, Dublin in reprisal for the murder of British intelligence officers.

But these events, grievous as they were to the Parkhead faithful, paled in significance in comparison with the apparent disappearance of Tommy McInally. Following his injury against Rangers, he had missed three games but then had returned in early November 1920 for two games against Kilmarnock and

Dumbarton in which he had played below his best and, most unusually, had failed to score. Then there was a very unfortunate game at Shawfield. It was meant to be a gala occasion for the opening of Clyde's new stand and it attracted a crowd of 20,000. Although McInally scored 'before the crowd had time to settle', Celtic then faded badly and lost the game 1–2. In the latter stages, coins and stones were thrown, one of them hitting a linesman and compelling Mr Commins himself, the manager of Clyde, to take over as linesman after having tried in vain to deliver a homily to the crowd to ask them to behave! *The Evening Times* gloated with a headline of 'How Are The Mighty Fallen' and a cartoon of a man with a Celtic strip drowning in the River Clyde, but also expressed a hope that the 'miscreant' who threw the coin at the linesman should be 'severely dealt with'.

McInally was presumably distressed by these events, but then for the following game he was nowhere in sight! The game on 27 November 1920 was a very easy 5–0 demolition of Raith Rovers at Parkhead. Tommy's replacement, Archie Longmuir, scored the first two goals and had a fine game as Celtic easily overpowered the Fifers, but that was not the main talking point among the fans. Where was McInally? What had happened? Celtic themselves gave no clue. Maley, normally so co-operative with the press and such a fine massager of bruised egos and charmer of newspaper reporters, was silent, and other players were obviously under orders to say nothing.

Wild rumours spread around Glasgow. McInally had been transferred or was about to be transferred to

Newcastle United or some other English club ... McInally was seriously ill following a drunken 'bender' ... McInally was known to be friendly with one of the illegal bookmakers and had placed a bet against Celtic in one or other of the recent games where Celtic had not done so well ... McInally had gone to Ireland to fight for independence ... McInally had struck Maley in a full and frank exchange of views – all these stories were told with certainty by someone who knew someone who told ... and were readily believed. That weekend Glasgow and Scotland talked about little other than Celtic's storm petrel, usually with what a later Celtic historian would describe as 'the argumentative certainty of the working class, where emphasis compensates for accuracy'.

The truth was bad enough, but a little more mundane. There had been what was termed an 'indiscretion' (presumably of a drunken nature) when the team was at Seamill Hydro in midweek. Hydro hotels, of course, did not sell alcohol – hence the reason for their popularity among football managers – but Tommy had presumably evaded the eagle eye of Maley for a spell to go out on the town. He had been caught and was given an informal suspension for a game by Maley who was of course all too aware of the prodigious talent of the boy and of his popularity with the supporters. Hence the relatively mild punishment and his prompt restoration to the team the following week.

The Evening Times reported that McInally 'rested' (not 'was rested') for the Raith Rovers game and predicted erroneously that he would not play in the next game. 'McInally, it is freely rumoured, has some alleged grievance and at any rate, he is not included in the Celtic team'. But the spirit of reconciliation was in the air and McInally and Maley made their peace on the Friday night before Saturday's game. It was as well that they did.

This game was against Falkirk on 4 December 1920 at an overcrowded Brockville and was heading for a 1–1 draw. The thousands who streamed out before the end of the game, an annoying habit of Celtic supporters which obtains even to this day, missed the two late goals from the apparently chastened Tommy McInally and the extravagant congratulations of Willie Maley. If Maley thought, however, that the prodigal son had returned for ever, he was in for a disappointment.

Elsewhere in the world a ship called 'The Celtic' had docked in New York with the widow of Terence McSweeney, the Lord Mayor of Cork who had died recently in Brixton Prison on hunger strike. Demonstrations of support for the Irish cause meant that when the band played the two national anthems, the American anthem was given a grudging reception but 'God Save The King' was drowned out by 'The Wearing Of The Green'!

Rangers' consistent form meant that Celtic were always struggling to catch up with them and the New Year was reached with Celtic six points behind. With only two points for a win in those days, this meant that Celtic would have to beat Rangers at Ibrox on New Year's Day, and then catch up another four points by winning the remainder of their games and hoping that another two teams could beat Rangers.

The New Year's Day game of 1921 has been immor-

talised by the descriptions of the brake clubs and charabancs coming back along Paisley Road with their flags,
banners, drums and bugles hailing the brilliance of
McInally and Gallacher and, in particular, the two goals
scored by Joe Cassidy. The second was a real beauty.
Patsy Gallacher beat three opponents, passed to
McInally who feinted to shoot, but cried 'Joe' as he did
and passed it to Cassidy who did the needful.
McInally's cry of 'Joe' was apparently heard in the press
box even above the noise of the crowd. Little wonder
then that the fans returned to the East End singing:

> We'll crown Joe Cassidy King of Ireland . . .
> And McInally the Prince of Wales!

McInally continued to shine throughout January and
February – a mild couple of months in 1921 when there
was very little disruption to the fixture list. Disturbingly,
the team had a couple of draws in January, in one of
which Tommy scored against Morton at Cappielow in
the rain, but then the following week at Motherwell, in
a blizzard, he failed to find the net, reflecting perhaps a
trend with Tommy, namely that he was not a good 'bad
weather' player. He scored a hat-trick against St.
Mirren, however, and could be relied upon to score
more often than not.

The Scottish Cup took Celtic to unusual territory in
Vale of Leven, a great team of the 1870s and 1880s but
now sadly in decline following the rise of professional-
ism, and to totally uncharted territory on 19 February at
East Fife, who went to the trouble of building an extra
embankment for the 10,000 crowd to see the wonders
of Tommy McInally. *The Leven Mail* told of the massive

Celtic following arriving by road and rail with 'horns, rattles and trumpets' and reported that they 'were under the usual impression of their type that the more noise they made, the greater the chances of victory for their team'. They certainly did make a great deal of noise when their hero Tommy McInally scored two goals in the 3–1 win as the team in general indulged in 'profitable passing and first time shooting'.

Perhaps the constant adulation went to his head or perhaps he began at this point to rebel against the basic-ally well-meaning but paternalistic Maley, but the spring saw a distinct tailing off in McInally's form. Four key games were lost, and in all of them the press either criticised McInally for having an 'off day', 'not looking like himself' or 'being out of sorts' or there was some-thing even worse – not being mentioned at all. A centre forward (although there were times when he seemed to be more of an inside forward) should really be noticed.

First the team exited the Scottish Cup in an unlucky performance at Parkhead against Hearts. This was on 5 March 1921, the day after there had been a political earthquake in the Kirkcaldy by-election when Tom Kennedy, the Labour candidate, had unseated the Coalition Liberal with the slogan of 'March forth on March fourth'. This news reached Glasgow just as the game was starting and the cheering reached a crescendo as the teams came out, Celtic without McNair or Cringan in the defence. It was a close game but Hearts went 2–1 up in the seventy-ninth minute before McInally had the mortification of seeing Joe Cassidy's shot hit the bar and his own header hit the underside of the bar in the very last minute. That would have earned the team a deserved replay at Tynecastle, but on such things does the Scottish Cup depend and it was not to be. A veteran supporter recalled some sixty years later how Tommy buried his head in his hands when his header came down off the bar, hit the line and was hooked clear by a Hearts defender. That night a sandwich board man was seen walking around the streets of Glasgow advertising *The Evening Citizen* with 'Labour triumph in Kirkcaldy' on the front and 'Celts Out As Tom Hits Bar' on the back.

Then there were two disastrous visits to Ayrshire to lose to Ayr United and then Kilmarnock which drastically undermined the championship challenge. This finally folded as the team lost to Raith Rovers in Kirkcaldy on 9 April. There was a certain excuse in the Ayr defeat, for there were several injuries and McStay and Cassidy were playing for the Scottish League, but in the other games there seemed to be little excuse. In the Raith Rovers game in particular, on the same day as Scotland were beating England 3–0 at Hampden, McInally was so overwhelmed by the Kirkcaldy centre half Dave Morris that questions were asked about whether Tommy's moment had passed.

But then, with the real damage done for the season, McInally came back to form. The penultimate league game of the season was against Hibs at Parkhead and McInally scored one of his sensational goals when he got the ball inside the centre area, charged through the Hibs defence, evading tackle after tackle then scoring himself – showing what he could do when he felt like it and raising the question of why he could not do it when it was required.

The Glasgow Charity Cup of 1921 was definitely McInally's. Celtic won the trophy by beating Partick Thistle 2–0 and then Rangers 2–0, and McInally scored all four goals. There was now a great danger of this trophy taking on a permanent green and white hue for Celtic had won it nine times out of the last ten! The final was played on 14 May 1921 against Rangers at Hampden before 50,000, a huge crowd when one considers that there was once again a rail strike and other transport problems. Labour problems were a constant feature of the 1920s of course but those who walked to Hampden in brilliant sunshine were well rewarded by two great McInally shots, one from a free kick, one from open play, but both earning the description of 'cannonballs'. Both were said to be deflections, but that mattered little to the delirious Celtic hordes who now had the last laugh in this otherwise depressing season.

The teams were:

Celtic: Shaw, McNair and Dodds; Gilchrist, McStay and McFarlane; McLean, Gallacher, McInally, Cassidy and Pratt.

Rangers: Robb, Manderson and McCandless; Meiklejohn, Dixon and Muirhead; Archibald, Cunningham, Henderson, Cairns and Morton.

The season thus finished on a high for Tommy, but the general feeling was that he had not made as much progress as one would have expected. True, he now possessed four winner's medals in the Glasgow competitions, but as yet nothing in a Scottish competition. Several games had shown him to be slow and he often had a tendency to fade the longer the game went on, particularly if things weren't going Celtic's way. His disappearance from the game in November had not gone unnoticed and rumours were already sweeping Glasgow about drunken over-indulgence.

To a certain extent, McInally suffered from 'second season syndrome', a phrase coined in the 1970s by English County Cricketers to explain the arrival of a talented youngster who is immediately hailed as a new Bradman or Boycott because of his fine displays. That is for his first season. By the second season, he has been 'sussed out' by opponents and a chastening reality check is delivered. This phenomenon happened with McInally in season 1920/21 but it is also true that he was already showing a disturbing ability to sow the seeds of his own downfall. 'But he is only young!', 'He will learn' said his apologists. Realists asserted that a hard kick up the bum might help him sort out his problems.

In the meantime an incident occurred in early summer 1921 in Glasgow which showed that the Irish troubles were none too far away from the Scottish mainland. An IRA suspect was being taken to Duke Street gaol from the Central Court, the van was hijacked and in the ensuing mayhem a policeman was shot. This was bad enough but what happened afterwards was shocking as scores of young Irishmen were arrested, detained and questioned, including a Roman Catholic priest from the Calton called Father McRory who was totally innocent. He was later released, but the incident did little to convince the Glasgow Irish that the police were in any way there to help or protect them.

McInally would have been very involved in all this (emotionally very sympathetic to the Irish cause if not actually physically involved in any protests or disturbances), for he never lacked passion about Irish politics. More importantly, his name would be much talked about by Father McRory in his wrongful imprisonment, for Soggarth Aroon (Our Beloved Priest), as McRory was known, was a regular visitor at Celtic Park and a great admirer of Tommy McInally.

The Celtic team themselves however, missed most of this for they went on tour to France and played their first game in Roubaix, which had been in German hands during the war. Visits were made to battlefields and wreaths laid on memorials. The games were mostly light hearted, but there was a game against Newcastle United won by Celtic so that the Magpies could see for themselves what they had missed in Tommy McInally, whose services they craved. On another occasion Tommy suffered from blisters in the heat and had to be moved to outside left where the long grass could cushion his feet! No indication exists of how well he behaved in the tour party but it seems to have been a fine experience for everyone and a great piece of propaganda for Celtic.

McInally's start to the 1921/22 season was delayed, for he was injured in pre-season training and out for virtually the whole month of August. September went tolerably well. He scored six goals and played his part in steering Celtic to the final of the Glasgow Cup on 1 October. It was this game that first saw Celtic fans begin to ask serious questions about Tommy McInally. A crowd of 76,878 were at Hampden to see Rangers score in the first ten minutes with a shot from right half Davie Meiklejohn. This need not have been fatal, for Celtic had plenty time to fight back and to claim their third successive Glasgow Cup.

But no fight-back came. Rangers remained on top and, but for Charlie Shaw in the Celtic goal, the score would have been a great deal more. Celtic had too many players who looked lethargic and uninterested, particularly McInally who seemed resigned to the defeat. To make matters worse, when the ball came to him he tried to show off with keepie-uppies and overdoing the bodyswerves. This sort of thing delighted his fans when the team were already well on top. In the circumstances of the team losing to Rangers in what was (in 1921) a major cup final, this did not come off. When the full-time whistle came, Tommy did not look nearly upset enough as he smiled his congratulations and shook hands with the Rangers defenders who could not believe that Tommy McInally had given them so little trouble.

Celtic fans will accept a defeat, but they will always find it difficult to accept inferior performances from a player whom they know can do better. They had seen McInally do so much better on previous occasions. The frustration which had been bottled all weekend came out in the next game played on the Tuesday immediately afterwards when St. Mirren came to Parkhead. The team played tolerably well and in fact won the game with goals from Joe Cassidy and Patsy Gallacher, but McInally again seemed out of sorts.

He showed a distinct reluctance to chase some balls, to display the speed for which he had become legendary and even seemed to have put on weight. No longer the lithe, agile, supple youth of two years previously, he looked unfit. The lovers of Tommy McInally looked on in despair as he failed to make any impact on a mediocre St. Mirren defence and the less patient of the crowd, having spent a weekend of having to thole the jeers of the Rangers fans, vented their spleen on McInally. Tommy then made matters worse, by pretending to put cotton wool in his ears and on one occasion to feign a run to the old pavilion in the North West corner of the ground. This nonsense singularly failed to impress and he finished the game a passenger on the left wing, having been told to exchange places with Archie Longmuir.

It was clearly time for manager Maley to 'have a word' with Tommy, who was beginning to tax his powers of tolerance and man-management. Maley's great side of the Edwardian era (less than two decades ago but now, seemingly, a different world considering all that had happened in the intervening time) had been a slick, cohesive outfit with many great players and, like Jock Stein's great side of the 1960s, not too dependent on any one player. They had also famously got on together with a notable lack of cliques. They were a team, not a collection of individuals. Tommy, however, was anything but a team man.

Yet there was something so likeable about the Barrhead boy ('I always had a soft spot for him' - Maley would say repeatedly) with no father and a perhaps too - demanding mother, that guaranteed that Maley would go the extra mile for him. Certainly hard discipline would not work, or at least, Maley felt that a softer approach should be tried first. It was like a priest talking to a penitent or a guidance teacher talking to a recalcitrant pupil.

Maley told him that his talent was immense, that the possibilities of playing for Scotland in international matches in front of six-figure crowds were there and that there really could be no limit to what he could achieve. Only Patsy Gallacher could be compared to him in terms of actual talent and potential . . . but at the moment, he was letting himself down by his over-indulgence in food and alcohol. More important than that, he was letting his fans down – his vast army of fans who, frankly, in some cases, had little going for them in their deprived, impoverished and under-privileged lives other than the love of Celtic Football Club. They paid a lot of money to come to Celtic Park to see him. Maley felt himself to be under pressure to drop him, but would not do so . . . for the moment. The remedy was in McInally's hands.

McInally went some way to redeeming himself in the eyes of his worshippers by scoring the goal at Ibrox which earned Celtic a 1–1 draw on 22 October and from then on throughout the winter, he toed the line. He scored a hat-trick (admittedly in a losing cause) against Kilmarnock and missed a few games in December through a bona fide injury (although he made a brave but misguided attempt to play in a point-less game against Rangers in the Unemployed Tournament, clearly believing that the unemployed, who would be admitted free, wanted to see him even if less than totally fit) but by the turn of the year was back in the Celtic team.

But rumours persisted that he was not happy, and that his team mates were not happy with him. In particular, the story that he and Patsy Gallacher did not get on refused to go away. There was no solid evidence to back it up but they were certainly two of a kind in both playing style and in temperament, and they were seen to shout at each other on the field when things were not going so well.

In addition, it was no secret that McInally was attracting the attention of a few English clubs, notably Newcastle United, Burnley and Chelsea. Celtic did little to discourage this, for they would have commanded a good price for Tommy and times were hard. In January 1922, when a representative from Chelsea saw Tommy score in Celtic's 2–0 win over Aberdeen at Parkhead, the Celtic Director Colonel John Shaughnessy refused to rule out the possibility of a deal, saying blandly, 'One never knows what will happen,' and McInally allowed himself to be quoted as saying that he was 'disheartened by the barracking', that he had a 'sensitive nature which was very susceptible to this unfair treatment'.

One presumes that this was said with tongue in cheek. Yet perhaps it wasn't, for often clowning is a cover for insecurity and no-one likes to feel that their efforts are not being appreciated. His remarks were certainly greeted with ridicule by the support, for the fact was that as long as Tommy produced the goods or even showed that he was trying his damnedest for the club, there would be no barracking. Certainly results continued to be respectable and the league challenge was maintained. McInally's two goals on St. Valentine's day against St. Mirren at Love Street, for example, put Celtic two points ahead of Rangers and things looked rosy for a spell.

Soon after this, Manchester City put in a bid for McInally, but the deal was scuppered by an unlikely source – Tommy's mother! Manchester City's manager Mr Ernest Magnall (McInally curiously called him 'Ted' Magnall) had been interested in McInally before, it will be remembered, and one day Tommy was summoned to Maley's 'The Bank' restaurant. Tommy, writing some thirty years later for the *Scottish Football Digest*, told the tale in his own inimitable style, occasionally, one feels, sacrificing truth to a fine piece of rhetoric or a telling phrase.

> The cash offered to me made me think of cruising in my own yacht in the Mediterranean. I came to the conclusion that my whack was just too good to miss, but there was one restraining thought: 'What would my mother say?' I explained that I wouldn't dream of leaving home without my mother's consent and departing from The Bank shortly after noon, I made for Barrhead. I returned to Messrs. Maley and Magnall a couple of hours afterwards with the information that my mother wished me to stay at home, and that was good enough for me. Mr. Magnall was a good talker but all the persuasive speeches in the world wouldn't have shifted me. I was adamant, despite the fact that I was told that never before had football heard of a player refusing such money as I was offered.

Disentangling the boasting and the exaggeration to find the truth is necessary here but three points do emerge.

One was that one of the wealthiest clubs in England was prepared to offer a king's ransom for the services of McInally; another is that McInally's mother had a tremendous influence on her beloved youngest son whom she did not want to lose to distant Manchester, believing perhaps that he lacked the maturity to cope with life without her; and the third was that Celtic were prepared to let him go at this point. Not surprisingly, Willie Maley does not mention this incident!

But then things took a disastrous turn when the Scottish Cup brought Hamilton Academical to Parkhead for what turned out to be the shock of the day and indeed the season. A crowd of 40,000 were there but long before half time boos rang out all round the ground for Hamilton, a team in the lower reaches of the First Division, incredibly, were 3–0 up. The goals had been scored by a fellow called Cottingham who had joined Hamilton from Parkhead Juniors and who lived near the ground. Celtic's only real effort had been a McInally shot which nearly 'wrenched the upright out of the ground, but which had then bounced clear'. This was too much for Maley who, frankly, blew his top and kept the team on the field at half time to give them a row. Fingers were pointed, gesticulations were made and Maley's voice was heard even in the crowd as McInally had to take his share of this public 'rollicking'.

McInally did not react well to this. He had been poor in the first half (although in all honesty he could not be blamed for the defence's shortcomings) and was worse in the second half, lethargic and lacklustre and unable to lead his line properly or even get a goal that would have brought Celtic back into the Scottish Cup. He had a few chances but his shooting was wayward. He was also lucky not to be sent off when 'he got Hunter with the toe of his boot' as *The Evening Times* coyly put it, but then went on to report, 'Hunter dropped like a brick, as did McMillan with no-one near him'. Joe Dodds eventually converted a penalty for Celtic in the last minute, but by that time Parkhead was an empty and silent place, Hamilton having won 3–1.

McInally was not, of course, the only culprit. Johnny Gilchrist and Willie Cringan would both leave the club, unhappy at the wages paid to them and at the tyranny of Maley; Patsy Gallacher had seemed moody and unhappy, but the general opinion of everyone seemed to be that the continuing presence of Tommy McInally was not a good thing for the team. He was too eccentric, too selfish, too argumentative, and Saturday had proved (as had the Glasgow Cup final in the autumn) that when he was required to do a job for the club he was found wanting. Celtic had thus gone out of the Scottish Cup at the quarter final stage in the three post-war seasons – a situation that the support found intolerable, and someone had to be blamed.

The fuming Maley picked virtually the same team to play the same opponents in a league match on the following Wednesday, 1 March – 'they got us into this mess, let them get us out!' – and they won 4–0 as it turned out, and McInally scored. He also picked up an injury and had to change places with Adam McLean who led the line well, and after that McInally disappeared from the scene.

From time to time, Maley would say something vague and non-committal about an injury, but this fooled nobody. McInally was either suspended or dropped. Any idea that he could have been injured was dispelled when he was allowed to play the first half of a benefit game at Cowdenbeath in early April before being 'substituted' by a local Fife boy called Lawrence Glancey who now played for Celtic. The vindictive Maley, feeling hurt and betrayed by McInally, knew how to humiliate!

Celtic now prospered, winning the league in breathtaking style without McInally at Morton at the end of April. Joe Cassidy had moved from inside left to centre forward to replace McInally and Cassidy's place had gone to a hard-working young Fifer called John McFarlane who would soon earn the unlikely nickname of 'Jean'. Celtic then went on tour to Czechoslovakia and Germany without McInally. What Tommy's feelings must have been, we can but imagine. Whenever we do find a newspaper reference to him, it is as the 'forgotten man of Parkhead'. What would have hurt him the most was the feeling that Celtic could live without him and that he had, temporarily at least, ceased to be the number one talking point of Glasgow.

This, one feels, was important for Tommy. All bad boys, as any teacher will confirm, love being the centre of attention, even though it is for something bad. In fact, it is often the case that it is the only way that they can command recognition in their emotionally deprived background. Ignoring them is just about the worst punishment that one can devise. Tommy was undeniably hurting and in these circumstances the 'siren song' attractions of the liquor became even more a part of his life. It was far too easy for the sociable and unmarried

Tommy to find his way to a pub where there would be no lack of people willing to buy him a whisky or a beer. And he was still only twenty-two!

While Tommy brooded in the summer of 1922, his mood not helped by the apparent lack of interest in him from other clubs, Celtic continued their policy of freezing him out. He was not listed by them for the following season and, as happened in those days, the Scottish League (whose President, ironically enough, was Willie Maley!) put him on the 'open to transfer list' with an asking price of £2,500. Still no-one came for him, whether deterred by the high asking price or by Tommy's now dreadful reputation. For public consumption Maley put out a story that McInally was making exorbitant wage demands. This however was not believed by anyone.

Partick Thistle may have been interested. McInally was certainly given permission to play for them at the Lochwinnoch Highland Games in a five-a-side tournament in late June. This was essentially a light-hearted affair, but used by players to keep up their fitness over the summer. In one of the games, as luck would have it, Partick Thistle were drawn to play Celtic whose five were Johnny Gilchrist, Patsy Gallacher, Joe Cassidy, Joe Dodds and Adam McLean. It may be that there was some attempt to 'get' McInally for a few dressing room old scores, and the game was played in a fashion distinctly out of tune for a relaxing summer occasion watched by families with children and gentlemen wearing kilts!

Joe Dodds (by coincidence not on Celtic's retained list either and using this opportunity to put a few goods in the shop window, as it were, for another club to examine) and McInally had a few jousts, verbal and otherwise, with each other before McInally scored for Thistle in a goal-mouth scramble. Dodds, the 'backing-in goalkeeper' (as it was termed in five-a-side) claimed that he was fouled and would not shut up about it. Goaded by McInally's taunts, Dodds continued his diatribe to such an extent that the referee had no option, even in these surroundings, but to send him off. Dodds refused to go, pointing out that reducing a team from five to four virtually condemned them to defeat, and when the referee was adamant, the remaining four Celts walked off the field as well, conceding the game to Partick Thistle and the mocking mirth of McInally.

This incident, insignificant in itself to anyone outside Lochwinnoch and reported with some levity and jesting in the few national papers which carried the story, nevertheless guaranteed that there could now be no possible way back for McInally at Parkhead. In any case Willie Crilly had been signed from Alloa for the 1922/23 season and was impressing the fans in the centre forward spot. But where was McInally to go? The fee of £2,500 was felt to be too high, and in any case, it was hard to imagine the totally Glaswegian Tommy playing for an English club or even someone like Aberdeen who had reputedly made an enquiry about him. So too, incredibly, and not for the first or last time, did Rangers.

Tommy himself in his memoirs told how 'an English manager' (annoyingly he does not say who) was interested in both himself and the great Hughie Ferguson of Motherwell. (Ferguson would, three years later in 1925, join Cardiff City and become 'the Scotsman who took the English Cup to Wales'. After that he returned to Dundee, suffered from depression and eventually committed suicide in January 1930). Tommy claims that he could have pocketed £1,300 – a huge sum of money in 1922 – but was reluctant to leave Barrhead and his mother who put all sorts of pressure on him to stay in the immediate neighbourhood, if he had to leave Celtic. It had never been heard of for a young lad to turn down so much money, but he did love Barrhead. He still, fairly obviously, loved Celtic as well.

In the end it was an approach from Alec Bennett, through intermediaries Joe McDevitt and Andrew Mitchell, which took Tommy away. Alec had played for Maley's great team until 1908 when he had moved to Rangers, had thus won league medals for both Celtic and Rangers, and was now manager of Third Lanark. Maley reckoned that, with McInally at Cathkin, Celtic would get the transfer fee and even if McInally returned to his best form, he would not hurt Celtic much in such a poor team as Thirds. So Maley agreed. Tommy accepted too, for the alternative was a premature end to a footballing career which had promised so much, and on Monday 4 September 1922, Tommy McInally signed for Third Lanark.

This event, perhaps inevitably, did not cause as much a stir as one might have expected. Obviously Celtic fans were disappointed but the loss of McInally did not seem to be all that significant considering that the team had won last year's League Championship without him in the latter stages. The start to the 1922/23 season had not been particularly impressive, however, and on the

Saturday before McInally's departure, the team, without McInally, had exited the Glasgow Cup to Queen's Park. But in any case there was another event which occurred that Monday that stunned the Celtic community even more. Sunny Jim Young, stalwart of the great Celtic teams from 1903 to 1916 as part of the immortal half back line of Young, Loney and Hay, and team mate of Alec Bennett, was killed in a tragic motor-cycling accident in Ayrshire. He sustained head injuries and died at 6.30pm that evening.

Parkhead and Maley were rocked by these three events of the Glasgow Cup exit, the death of the legendary Sunny Jim and the McInally transfer. The team would take all year and more to recover. Tommy however faced a new beginning.

4

Pining for Home

Third Lanark are sadly no longer with us as a senior team. In recent years there has been an amateur team of that name playing at Cathkin Park but the senior outfit went to the wall in 1967, victims of desperate mismanagement and sometimes sheer corruption. Ironically, the same year saw a Glasgow team, Celtic, win the European Cup, another Glasgow team, Rangers, reach the final of the European Cup Winners' Cup, yet another Glasgow team, Clyde, reach the dizzy heights of being third in Scotland and Scotland themselves record their famous 3–2 win against England at Wembley. It was a great time to be a Scottish football fan, except for poor old Thirds.

Stories abound about Thirds' last few years and the desperate poverty that engulfed them. They could not afford a new ball for a game – and had to paint an old one! On another occasion they began with an undersized ball blown up by an old bicycle pump to look like the appropriate size – and it burst with the first solid kick! On a return from an away fixture in Aberdeen, a battered old minibus stopped outside a fish and chip shop in Forfar and a director bought fifteen fish suppers out of his own pocket to feed the players.

Yet it was not always so. Although possibly the poorest (economically) of the six Glasgow teams, Third Lanark produced many fine players, like goalkeeper Jimmy Brownlie, Neil Dewar, Jimmy Mason, Ally MacLeod, Matt Gray, Alec Harley and many others who graced the game in almost 100 years of existence. Their ground, Cathkin, still exists, a short walk away from Hampden Park, an evocative trip for the historian and a potent reminder of how football teams must budget properly and not allow themselves to slip into careless or dangerous hands.

In 1922, Third Lanark had a reasonable support averaging out at 8,095, and shared the south side catchment area with Queen's Park, tending to have a slightly more working-class fan base than the somewhat patrician Queen's Park did but enjoying a healthy rivalry with them. The grounds of Celtic and Clyde were not all that far away either and as long as football remained healthy, Thirds' existence would be guaranteed. It was only in the 1960s, when influences like television began to affect football, that Third Lanark began to suffer. Paradoxically, it was because the working man had become more prosperous. He could now afford other things as well, and it became apparent that Glasgow could not sustain six football teams.

But in playing terms, even by 1922 when Tommy joined Thirds, their best years were behind them. They had won the Scottish Cup in 1889 and 1905 and the Scottish League in 1904 (beautifully told in a fine book *Third Lanark – Champions of Scotland 1903–04* by

Thomas Taw) under a manager with the unlikely name of Frank Heaven, but other successes were scarce. In autumn 1908 they had beaten the great Celtic team 4–0 in the third attempt to play the Glasgow Cup final (a result which raised a few eyebrows at the time) but since then their position had been mediocre. They had kept going during the difficult days of the war and had usually finished up in the middle of the table. Their subsequent history after the McInally triennium from 1922 to 1925 would be one of sad under-performance. They would win the Glasgow Cup and the Glasgow Charity Cup once each, reach the final of the Scottish Cup in 1936 and the Scottish League Cup in 1959 . . . but that was all.

Their manager in 1922 was an interesting character called Alec Bennett. Alec is generally regarded as being one of the best right wingers that Scotland have ever had, earning the nickname of the 'artful dodger', as he won four Scottish League medals with Celtic in the legendary Bennett, McMenemy, Quinn, Somers and Hamilton forward line, then jumped ship to Rangers and won another three Scottish League medals there. He also won eleven Scottish caps and two Scottish Cup medals.

The amazing thing about Bennett was that he never seems to have been pilloried the way that Mo Johnston and Kenny Miller were for crossing the Old Firm divide. Certainly in the years before the Great War, the religious divide was not as great as it became later but the move was still an astonishing one, for in 1908 when he joined Rangers, Celtic had won every trophy on offer and were generally regarded as the best in the world.

Possibly, as a non-Catholic, Bennett felt ill at ease at Parkhead. Certainly David McLean, another Protestant who played for Celtic at the time, complained about being constantly harrassed by priests and nuns to make charitable contributions but, on the other hand, that seemed to present no problem for Jimmy Young or Jimmy Hay or Eck McNair. Maybe Bennett fell out with the autocratic Maley, or possibly he just happened to like Rangers. Certainly, there seems to be no evidence of any sustained ill feeling towards him from either set of supporters.

Alec was a gentle, loveable man, very fond of football, whose appointment at Third Lanark in August 1921 was greeted with joy throughout Glasgow. He must have known what he was letting himself in for in the signing of Tommy McInally in 1922 but the general feeling was that it would do the talented Tommy some good to have a change. It was generally accepted that Tommy was too fond of Glasgow and was too much part of Glasgow culture to want to leave the city (both Aberdeen and Newcastle maintained an interest in him) and here was a new opportunity for him. He also had very strong family links to keep him in Glasgow, as we have seen.

The Glasgow Herald predicted that the 'arrival of Tom McInally will attract many spectators to the south side enclosure for Saturday's game against Hamilton', but the news tended to be buried under events like the death of Sunny Jim and the ongoing violence in Ireland where two members of the 'National Army' (Free State) had been shot dead and another ten injured in an IRA ambush in Cork as they stood in front of Cork City Chambers in a queue awaiting their pay.

As it happened, McInally did not play against Hamilton on Saturday, probably because it was felt by the Third Lanark management that he was not quite fit enough yet, and thus his debut was delayed until the following week when Rangers went to Cathkin for the Glasgow Cup semi final. A crowd of 37,000 were there in spite of dreadful wind and rain to see a spirited 2–2 draw in which Thirds were 0–2 down but McInally pulled one back before Reid scored at the very end after most of the crowd had gone home thinking that Rangers had won.

He then played against St. Mirren on the following Saturday, missing a good chance as the poor Third Lanark team went down 1–3, but then he played well the following Wednesday against Rangers in the replayed semi final at Ibrox before 30,000, scoring Thirds' only goal in the narrow 1–2 defeat. Yet phrases like 'McInally's lone furrow' in press reports indicate that there was a lack of cohesion in the team.

The pattern in his early games tended to be that although Tommy made an impact on the Cathkin side, he suffered in that he lacked support from the rest of the fairly poor Third Lanark forward line. On 21 October he found himself up against his brother Arthur, now the centre half of newly promoted Alloa Athletic. Arthur had had a varied career since he turned out for Celtic on one occasion during the war, having plied his trade for Ayr United, St. Mirren, Abercorn and Dunfermline, but had now settled down to play well for Alloa. The press reported some 'interesting bouts' between the brothers McInally, but Arthur must have had the last laugh for Alloa won 1–0 at Cathkin.

Tea time conversation would have been interesting in Barrhead that night!

Saturday 25 November 1922 gave Celtic fans a chance to welcome back their errant child. Celtic's form had been poor. Already out of the Glasgow Cup by the time that McInally had left, and complaining bitterly and permanently about poverty, they were also struggling in the league, having lost the previous week to Airdrie. Third Lanark were faring little better, having lost to Raith Rovers a couple of weeks previously and only drawn with Falkirk the week before as the McInally magic conspicuously failed to materialise. On this day at Parkhead, Tommy was totally anonymous, 'disappearing into the pocket of Willie Cringan' as Celtic beat Third Lanark 3–0 with a hat-trick from Joe Cassidy.

The Scottish Cup saw a good run by the 'warriors' in 1923. The first round on 13 January paired Third Lanark with Partick Thistle at Firhill. This was a Glasgow derby, of course, and although it lacked the huge crowd and atmosphere of other Glasgow derbies, it was nevertheless a closely fought tussle. The first game at Firhill saw honours even with a 1–1 draw and a replay therefore at Cathkin the following Tuesday afternoon – a game which drew a fair crowd of 15,000. Thirds would win through but not without a little gamesmanship or even perhaps outright cheating from Tommy McInally.

He was running in on goal and four Partick Thistle defenders converged on him, thereby blocking the view of the referee. Tommy was tackled and went down screaming in agony claiming that he had been kicked.

All the Partick Thistle defenders denied this but Tommy was a consummate actor and a penalty kick was awarded as the stretcher was called for. The apparently badly injured McInally kept saying that his leg was broken. As Tommy was carried off, Third Lanark took the penalty, Bobby Orr netted, Tommy suddenly sat up on the stretcher, said 'thank you' to the stretcher bearers for their time, ran back on the field and congratulated Bobby Orr. This incident would not have been allowed today, one feels, but the referee saw nothing wrong with it that day in 1923. Third Lanark went on to win the game 3–2 and relationships between Tommy McInally and Partick Thistle took a long time to heal. Another incident with Tommy and Partick Thistle several years later would guarantee that he would never become one of Maryhill's favourite sons.

Thirds were now on a roll and on 20 January 1923 a purposeful Thirds team beat Celtic 1–0 at Cathkin. This game was remarkable for marking the debut of a nervous young Celt called Jimmy McGrory. Thirds looked far more confident than they had on their visit to Parkhead last November and McInally showed some of his old sparkle as Willie Hillhouse, whom they had signed from Albion Rovers, scored the only goal of the game. Celtic on the other hand were in even more trouble with internal dissension. John Gilchrist looked half fit in this game, did not turn up for training on the following Monday complaining of a poisoned knee, was suspended on the Tuesday and sold to Preston North End for £4,500 on the Friday. Many Celtic supporters were now calling unambiguously for the recall of McInally.

But Third Lanark had a good Scottish Cup run that season, reaching as far as the semi final. The semi was reached not without a struggle, however, for after the replay to defeat Partick Thistle, another replay was needed to beat the struggling Second Division team Vale of Leven. They then excelled themselves to beat strong going Ayr United but the quarter final draw paired them against Dundee, currently several places above Thirds in the league.

Dundee were a strong side but had foolishly sold their star left winger Alec Troup to Everton earlier in the year and had since faltered. It was nevertheless expected that they would be too good for Thirds even at Cathkin. 39,000 (an astonishingly large crowd but indicative of the love of Scottish Cup football at the time) were at Cathkin to see a 1–1 draw. Thirds should have won and would have done so if their forwards had been more active in supporting McInally who was 'the danger man of the quintet'. The following Wednesday afternoon a large contingent of Thirds fans travelled to Dundee where 20,000 (the *Dundee Advertiser* could not understand where they all came from) saw a goalless draw with neither centre forward – McInally of Thirds nor David McLean (who had once understudied Jimmy Quinn at Celtic and who, as we have seen, was quite glad to leave Parkhead where he was pestered by priests) of Dundee – able to make any impact. The tie now went to a third game, this time at neutral Ibrox on Tuesday 6 March when over 31,000 saw McInally at last get the better of the mighty Dyken Nicoll and put the Cathkin men into the semi final.

The Redcoats (one of the many nicknames bestowed

on Third Lanark – the Sodgers, the Warriors, the Hi Hi Hi's being some of the others) scarcely had time to draw breath for the semi finals were on the following Saturday – Thirds v Hibs at Tynecastle and Celtic v Motherwell at Ibrox. Thirds might have hoped for a venue in Glasgow but as Celtic and Motherwell were already at Ibrox it was felt that Edinburgh deserved the other semi.

The 49,000 crowd (the second-largest crowd Thirds had ever played in front of, beaten only by the Scottish Cup final of 1905) contained many Glasgow fans who had travelled through on the Football Specials and Tynecastle looked dangerously overcrowded as the teams took the field. Unfortunately for the Cathkin men, Hibs scored in the first minute of the game when red-haired Jimmy Dunn netted a rebound from a free kick which the goalkeeper had parried. The 'capitalists' (the name given to any of the Edinburgh sides, rather than a Marxist comment on rich people) then took a hold of the game, deploying their offside trap to perfection against the 'brilliant' Third Lanark inside trio of Reid, Walker and McInally. There was no further scoring and thus Tommy was deprived of a chance to play in a Scottish Cup final which would have set Scotland alight. The opponents would have been none other than Celtic. As it was, Tommy's old friend Joe Cassidy scored the only goal of that game against Hibs in a dull final.

Third Lanark finished fourth bottom in the league that season. McInally had been inconsistent, but not without his good moments. On 17 February, for example, he scored twice in a 3–1 win over Hearts at

Cathkin, but too often he was anonymous, occasionally lightening a dull ninety minutes with a flash of genius but otherwise mired in the grim struggle to avoid relegation. But he remained a personality and when the Langbank Home invited the St. Rochs junior team to play a scratch Celtic XI on 7 May 1923, who else would they invite to be the referee but Tommy McInally? It was an occasion which he milked to the utmost.

A week later, Tommy took part in one of the greatest adventures of Scottish football up to that time when a Third Lanark party, with a few guests, sailed to South America on tour. Leaving on 16 May on the luxury liner *Gelria* and not returning until 4 August (just in time for the start of the new season) the bold Scottish adventurers played eight games, won four, drew two and lost two. This tour had been arranged as early as the previous October by the enterprising Alec Bennett and although many Scottish teams had been to Europe before (Thirds themselves had been to Portugal in 1912), some of the Scottish press felt that South America was just a little too far away. The guests taken along to supplement Third Lanark and to allow them to claim (bogusly) that this team was the 'pick of Scotland' included Hughie Ferguson of Motherwell, Tom Ferguson and Tommy Glancy of Falkirk, Willie Frame of Motherwell and Bobby Archibald of Raith Rovers.

It was an eye-opening experience, but in spite of the hostile atmosphere in some grounds, Third Lanark were made very welcome by the Scottish ex-pats and their Argentine hosts. This tour was historically significant in that it played a large part in the development of Argentinian football, for the Argentinians looked upon

Scottish football as the best in the world (as it probably was in the 1920s). McInally scored three goals and was able to charm even the most volatile of South American fans who laughed at the antics of 'El Tommy', both on and off the field. No evidence exists of how Tommy behaved, but it would be a fair guess that he had his 'moments'.

The first game was played against an 'Argentine XI' in Palermo. What shocked the Scots players was not so much the rabid crowd of 20,000, the scores of armed police or the wire fence which separated the crowd from the players, as the reaction to an erroneous refereeing decision to award a corner kick. While Scottish crowds might well have hurled abuse at the official, the temperamental Argentinian crowd hurled bottles, knives and even fired guns! Although the Scots were reassured by the police after they had made a tactical retreat to the pavilion that the gun firing was 'of no significance', they took a little persuasion to go back out again, but then tactfully Bobby Archibald, on McInally's advice, deliberately made a mess of the corner kick and the crowd settled down, even applauding when Third Lanark eventually won.

On another occasion, Tommy had to use all his wits and ability against a burly Brazilian defender – not to score goals against him, but to avoid being maimed by some of his tackles and charges that were more like assaults. Tommy dodged him time and time again, earning bullfighting-type cries of 'Ole, Mally!' from the appreciative crowd who couldn't quite say 'McInally', before eventually getting fed up of it and stopping to pick up the ball and give it to the none-too-intelligent Brazilian on the grounds that if he wanted the ball as badly as all that, he could have it! The crowd roared with laughter.

Some Argentinians were not too impressed with the whole tour, however. *The Buenos Aires Herald*, for example, told its readers that Third Lanark were a failure in that they passed on 'none of their professional excellence' to the Argentine amateurs. They 'held their own and nothing more'. *El Telegrafo* was even more direct as it remonstrated with the Cathkin men: 'Your play, your manners and your tactics disappointed us and our people, and we are sure that if you prolonged your stay here and took part in our first division championship, you would lose more than one game'. It then politely said that there was nothing personal in all this, but for 150,000 US Dollars, the Argentinian people deserved more. It then ended up by saying, 'Once more, good-bye, Scots players'.

The reference to the team's 'manners' may mean that some of the players may have over-indulged themselves in the local hospitality, and it would be hard to believe that McInally was not part of that, but the truth was that Third Lanark were not a great side, even with the addition of a few players from other teams. The tour ended with the team being caught in a typhoon ('It wasn't all that bad,' said McInally. 'When I was wi' Celtic, I saw Maley in a bad mood after we goat bate!') just as they were about to leave Buenos Aires on the *Highland Pride* and then they travelled homewards, befriending and playing cards with a couple of men, unaware that one of them had just been arrested for fraud and that the other was a Scotland Yard man who had just done the arresting!

The tour did have one effect on McInally, however, and that was that he appreciated that the South Americans were good ball players. It had been the fashion in Scotland, and would continue to be the fashion for many years, to dismiss South Americans as foppish theatrical entertainers rather than football players. Tommy was not of that persuasion and warned Scotland repeatedly about how good Uruguay would be when they played Scotland in the World Cup in 1954. However, his siren voice was ignored and Uruguay won 7–0.

Certainly the tour seemed to have a deleterious effect on the start of the 1923/24 season, for Third Lanark only had time for one practice match before the season started, missing even the Rangers and the Celtic Sports five-a-side tournaments. They lost 1–4 to Hibs in their first game (McInally scoring the consolation goal from a penalty kick) and did not win a league game until 6 October when they beat Hearts 2–1. Since the start of the season, they had gone down at home to Hibs, Morton and Partick Thistle and eked out a 0–0 draw with Airdrieonians while their away form had seen defeats at Dundee and local rivals Queen's Park. Yet, paradoxically, they had done well in the Glasgow Cup, reaching the final of that tournament in what would be their biggest game since the end of the war.

Sadly, the Hi Hi Hi's were outclassed by a rampant Rangers side on 29 September and were lucky to get away with a 3–1 defeat. The game was played at Ibrox rather than neutral Hampden or Parkhead and home advantage was probably significant. It was a dull, drizzly, misty day which reduced the crowd to 25,000 and the takings to £927. McInally actually scored first, (at the second attempt, having miskicked first) and Thirds fans were anticipating an unlikely and rare victory as the teams changed round at half time, but in the second half Rangers took control and goals from Tommy Muirhead, Sandy Archibald and George Henderson sealed their fate.

The first league win of the season against Hearts seems to have owed a little to the arrival of an old team mate of Tommy's, Willie Cringan, a Scotland cap and centre half and captain of Celtic. He too had fallen foul of Willie Maley at Parkhead but for different reasons from McInally. Cringan had led a dignified protest about bonus payments, (something that Maley had considered subversive), and had been dropped, then transferred for £1,200. Celtic's folly was Thirds' gain and the form of the Cathkin men temporarily improved.

But it did not seem that way the following week, when the team went to Kirkcaldy to be on the wrong end of a 6–1 beating from a truly great Raith Rovers side. McInally 'showed real cleverness' but was clearly upset at the rest of his team who, frankly, were not in the same category as McInally for footballing ability. In spite of that, however, the team then began to rally and a few hard-fought wins were eked out against teams like Aberdeen and Clyde.

But McInally was now on the skids again, not taking himself seriously, not training as hard as he could, so that he very often 'disappeared' from a game shortly after half time. A case in point was the visit to Celtic Park on 1 December. Tommy had a good enough first half and played a part in the goal scored by Willie Reid which reduced the deficit from 0–2 to 1–2. But then after Patsy Gallacher had put Celtic 3–1 ahead, McInally visibly lost interest in the game. His heart, in all truth, was not in it. He would much rather be playing for the other side and, misjudging the mood of the minuscule Celtic crowd (as low as 2,000 according to some reports) tried to clown and show off. His antics were greeted with silent indifference from the crowd (who were enjoying a rare good Celtic performance) and hostile contempt from his own team mates. Following more of the same half-heartedness the following week against Motherwell (even though the team won the game), manager Alec Bennett had to drop McInally.

But Tommy was always prepared to show contrition when he had to, and soon after New Year 1924 he was back, playing respectably in a losing cause when Celtic came to Cathkin in early January and earning an un-official 'man of the match' in the Scottish Cup on 26 January 1924 when Thirds drew 0–0 with Hearts. The press described him as the 'best man afield' and said that only 'cruel luck' stopped him from scoring on more than one occasion. Thirds' earning of a replay, however, did them little good when they went down 0–3 to Hearts in the following midweek.

Leisure from Cup ties then allowed Celtic and Third Lanark to play a bizarre friendly in which there were two referees. This had been an idea much put about by Willie Orr, a team mate and friend of Alec Bennett in their pre-war Celtic days. Orr was now the manager of the fine Airdrie team and being much respected in Scottish footballing circles, his idea was tried out. It was never tried again and McInally was not involved in this game of the two referees. 'I would be bound to get in trouble wi' the baith o' them,' he joked.

There could be no escaping the conclusion that Third Lanark were a poor side, locked in a relegation battle with two other Glasgow sides, Queen's Park and Clyde, and the Clydebank side for whom Jimmy McGrory was on loan. Indeed it was at the Clydeholm ground on 1 March against Clydebank that McInally turned on his best performance that season when, in an amazing spell of fifteen minutes, he scored four goals! This 'McInally's Hurricane', as *The Evening Times* put it, was the sort of display that made people think that McInally on his day could be one of the best players on earth. The sad thing was that these days did not come round very often.

Indeed we find even a few days later against Falkirk (a game that Thirds won 2–1) that 'McInally alone had at least half a dozen dead snips and missed in a manner which would have disgraced a schoolboy'. He then missed a couple of games through injury before returning to play against Rangers on 22 March. He was injured again, went to the wing (no substitutes in those days) and then failed to reappear for the second half as the team lost 1–2.

Third Lanark eventually saved themselves from relegation that season with a 2–2 draw at Motherwell on Saturday April 19 1924, followed by a 3–2 defeat of Hamilton at Cathkin a couple of days later on the Monday. McInally played in both these games and scored in both, so can claim to have played a great part in saving Thirds from relegation, finishing just ahead of

Clyde. It all happened over the Easter weekend. On Good Friday, champions Rangers lost 1–3 at Shawfield to Clyde, a result that raised eyebrows and looked to Thirds supporters like a 'fix'. On the Saturday as Airdrie were winning the Scottish Cup by beating Hibs, Thirds were two up over Motherwell (Tommy scored with a great drive) but then allowed Motherwell to equalise and earn a draw. Thus Easter Monday saw Clyde and Thirds level on points as they went into their last game. Clyde could only draw 2–2 with Hearts and Thirds were being held by Hamilton at the same score before Tommy McInally justified his wages by popping up to score a late winner.

Tommy had every reason to be pleased with this season. Saving Third Lanark from relegation was an achievement that he valued almost as much as his successes in the Glasgow tournaments for Celtic. But rescuing a team from relegation is at best a hollow triumph. What he really craved was national success. This was frankly unlikely with Third Lanark and it would only happen for Tommy if he managed to get back to Celtic. But they too were in disarray at the end of the 1923/24 season, their worst season since before the War.

Third Lanark may have been saved from relegation for a season but it still meant the end of the line for the kindly Alec Bennett who resigned as manager a month later alleging inability to pick the team that he wanted. He then moved on to Clydebank. It may be that Bennett was finding McInally a little too hot to handle but found himself in a cleft stick, for he could neither drop nor sack McInally who was Thirds' only player of real talent. But Bennett had at least tried to work with McInally. His successor would be less willing to do so.

Bennet would be replaced by John Richardson, who had been in charge of Petershill junior club and then Raith Rovers for a short spell during the Great War. He would be a lot less tolerant of McInally's foibles than Bennett had been. There were other changes too. Willie Cringan, who had done so much to shore up a leaky defence, was also on his way to Motherwell but Third Lanark's reputation for being a home for discontented Celts was enhanced when Johnny Gilchrist joined the club. This was not a good decision, for Gilchrist, a notorious trouble maker at Celtic, had been perpetually in bother at Preston North End and was currently on loan at Carlisle.

Gilchrist did little for the club. He was soon dismissed as being 'palpably inefficient' and disappeared to Dunfermline as season 1924/25 turned out to be a horror story for both McInally and Third Lanark. McInally was more or less permanently in trouble with the new manager and the Cathkin side found themselves relegated for the first time in their existence. McInally, blatantly unhappy where he was, was forever being linked with a transfer. Several English clubs watched him but he still evinced no strong desire to cross the border. There was little doubt that he was 'working his ticket' to return to Parkhead.

Tommy himself, writing in a magazine called *The Scottish Football Digest* in October 1949, tells a story which one presumes refers to this time of his career. It is typical McInally in the sense that it is all about himself and one must be very careful before one believes every word that he says for it reflects little credit on himself, showing himself to be boorish, ill-mannered and ill-disciplined. It is little surprise that he did not stay long at Third Lanark after this – if the story is to be believed at all! He ranted about the uselessness of coaches and theorists and said:

> I recall an incident in my playing days ... not with Celtic. The manager and directors called a meeting with the players, and we trooped in to see a board laid out as a football pitch with eleven corks positioned after the fashion of a team's line-up. While the players stood around, the directors commenced to move the corks about, giving what they erroneously believed were examples of good positional play. A cork would be moved from inside-right to inside-left, and so on. This ridiculous performance went on for about fifteen minutes, and I could stand it no longer. I flicked the board and the corks into the air, and remarked to the rest of the players,'Come on hame. The other team has scored.'

We must, of course, take this story with a pinch of salt, but if it has any grain of truth in it, we can see why Tommy was such a difficult fellow to manage and why his days at Third Lanark would be numbered.

The Glasgow Cup semi final on 20 September 1924 against Celtic would be an excellent chance for him to show off his qualities with a view to getting his obvious wish for a return. Now more or less permanently at inside left, where it was felt that his creative qualities would be most obvious, he was heavily involved in Third Lanark's first goal, although the normally mild-mannered Charlie Shaw claimed that McInally fouled him as Walker scored. So incensed was Charlie that he chased famous referee Peter Craigmyle back to the centre line to protest and returned to his goal scowling at the grinning McInally. But that was all that McInally did that day. For the rest of the game he was well shackled by a prodigiously talented youngster called Peter Wilson and Celtic won 4–2 with another youngster, Jimmy McGrory, scoring twice.

Trouble dogged McInally that season. Not all of it was his own making, for he had an injured shoulder, but he hardly endeared himself to his team mates or the Cathkin supporters by not going, when out injured, to Dundee with the team on 1 November and appearing instead at the Morton v Celtic match. Morton won 1–0, the crowd caused trouble and young McGrory was carried off. It was not a great day for Celtic, but McInally was keen to remind everyone of his existence and may well have thought that if McGrory was to be out of action there might be a void for him to fill. Rumours began to be spread, quite deliberately by McInally and his friends, around Glasgow.

But when Celtic went to Cathkin three weeks later, McInally was still at Thirds and still not happy. He was in trouble between Christmas and New Year for 'bad timekeeping on a league trip to Aberdeen' and it would not have taken a huge leap of imagination to guess that there might have been some alcohol involved. If he was trying to catch Maley's eye, McInally was going about it the wrong way, and his behaviour in the Celtic v Third Lanark game in early January really defies analysis.

The game was at Parkhead on Monday 5 January 1925. Celtic had been having a desperately awful New Year, losing heavily to Rangers and Airdrie. Thirds, on the other hand, had delighted their supporters with a 3–0 win over Partick Thistle at Firhill on New Year's Day but had then gone down 0–2 to St. Johnstone two days later. Very soon, against an understrength Third Lanark side for whom McInally looked grossly unfit and did not even seem to be trying, Celtic found themselves 2–0 up. The referee, Mr Russell, had awarded Celtic a penalty kick for the second goal and there had been a mild, restrained and dignified Third Lanark protest. But the penalty stood and Willie McStay converted.

The game continued but then there was a mild scuffle between two players – what was termed in 1920s journalese as a 'throw-up'. It was probably nothing more than a square up, but as Mr Russell tried to separate the two players, McInally ran up and tripped up the luck-less official! To say that this was bizarre behaviour was putting it mildly – *The Glasgow Herald*, in a turn of phrase that no-one would use today, described it as 'interfering with the referee' – and Tommy had to be sent off. This was the day that he made his poor joke about 'I'd rather go to the Empire' when told to go to the pavilion, and all that this incident did was turn McInally, once again, into a national talking point and even laughing stock.

It is of course possible that Tommy was drunk and there were certainly serious repercussions. Celtic went on to win 7–0 (Thirds' left back Higgins was carried off, so they finished with only nine men); Tommy was given a lengthy suspension, thereby missing the Scottish Cup tie between the teams which Celtic won easily, and the Third Lanark establishment now looked for a way to get rid of Tommy McInally. Had they not been in such dire straits about relegation he would almost certainly have been sacked. As it was, he was used sparingly for the rest of the season, although he did score a couple of goals against Hearts to earn a draw in mid February.

It was now certain that Tommy's days at Cathkin were numbered but the big question was whether the authoritarian Maley would accept him back at Celtic. Indeed, what about the other Celtic players who had felt let down by him in 1922, and what would the support feel about him? They all loved Tommy the man, but was Tommy the player, the one who had let himself down so badly in the game of 5 January and on numerous other occasions, able to produce the goods for Celtic? Tommy loved the Celtic, of that there was little doubt, and he would no doubt promise to reform and toe the line, but was he able to deliver on that promise?

At several points during the season (indeed ever since 1922) newspapers hinted at a return to Parkhead for Tommy McInally. 'Celtic are interested in a Third Lanark forward' would be juxtaposed beside a picture of Tommy McInally and a mention of his unhappiness at Cathkin. Willie Maley himself, without saying anything outright, would encourage this speculation by himself dropping hints: 'I have worried over Tommy, but when all is said and done, all his faults and foibles weighed up, I could never overcome a personal regard for this big, laughter-making boy from Barrhead who was out-and-out a Celt, and I am sure of this – that Tommy McInally in his pondering periods regrets very sincerely his premature departure from Parkhead.'

As winter gave way to spring in 1925, however, events took a bizarre twist when reports began to appear in various newspapers that Rangers were interested in signing Tommy McInally. *The Barrhead News*, for example, talked about the 'local crack football player' possibly joining Rangers. This story was also carried by some (but not all) the national dailies, and around the middle of March 1925, various reports appeared to the effect that 'it is now certain that McInally will sign for Rangers'. More than eighty years later this seems unlikely on several counts and it may be that it was a deliberate false lead by Rangers to upset Celtic before the imminent Scottish Cup semi final between the two teams.

There was, for one thing, the matter of religion. Roman Catholics had played for Rangers in the past – Willie Kivlichan, for example, and indeed McInally himself had had a few trials in the 1918/19 season – and there was as yet no hard and fast rule (lamentably, there soon would be) that Rangers were an all-Protestant team, but a Roman Catholic playing for Rangers in 1925 would be unusual, to put it mildly. No player of that faith had donned the colours in recent years. There were two key differences between 1919 and 1925. One was that the club was now in the hands of William Struth, a hard and determined character, as distinct from the more likeable William Wilton. The other difference was the Rangers management's lamentable bowing to the prejudices of the Ulster protestants who now worked in the Clyde shipyards, brought their loathsome mythologies with them, and found themselves welcomed with open arms by the Church of Scotland.

An even stronger objection to McInally joining Ibrox would appear to lie in the character of Rangers' manager. Struth was nicknamed 'God's truth' and

'Ruthless Struth', and was notoriously strict in the disciplining of players who even had to turn up for training well dressed. Struth insisted on collar and tie and even, on occasion, bowler hats! There would be little tolerance for McInally's slack habits and his well known fondness for the 'demon drink' in the calvinistic ambience of presbyterian Rangers.

A few Rangers sources at this point said that the real objection to McInally joining Rangers came from the Rangers players themselves. To an extent this is inevitable because no player really wants to see a well-known player from another club joining them. It is, of course, a threat to their position, so Andy Cunningham or Tommy Cairns might have orchestrated a campaign against McInally joining them. But there was also a general feeling from other members of the Rangers team, including those not directly threatened by the arrival of McInally, that he might cause dressing room trouble. Scottish football being the incestuous, gossipy world that it was, their friends at both Celtic and Third Lanark would have told them of the strife and grief that he had caused in both these places.

In addition, there was enough evidence to suggest that in 1925 McInally would simply have been a bad buy because he was failing to produce the goods on the playing field. Being the best known personality in Glasgow did not make Tommy a good player. His career so far had been one of comparatively unfulfilled potential. The ability was certainly there. The performances had not so far matched the ability – or rather had not matched the ability on a consistent basis. At that moment he was doing nothing to deserve the attention of Rangers and it is hard to imagine where he would have fitted in to the fine team that Rangers had in 1925.

For whatever reason, nothing came of it and *The Glasgow Observer* was able to re-assure 'those of the Ibrox faithful who are up against the co-opting of Tommy McInally by the Rangers may sleep soundly tonight. There will be no transfer.' There may have been nothing there in the first place. It may even be that the story came in the first instance from McInally himself with his irresistible urge to be the number one topic of Glasgow and Scottish conversation. Perhaps it was merely a story fabricated by some journalist to fill pages on a dull day, or it may have been a silly story that someone 'overheard in a pub' and soon developed a life of its own! To this day Glasgow remains a hot bed of footballing gossip – and if a story isn't true, does that matter?

But Glasgow now had another topic of conversation and that was the semi final of the Scottish Cup between Celtic and Rangers. Rangers were everyone's favourites but had a hoodoo in the Scottish Cup, which they had not won since 1903. A six-figure crowd turned up at Hampden on 21 March 1925 – and one of them was Tommy McInally. On the day when Third Lanark were beaten 8–0 at Motherwell, and more or less condemned to relegation, Tommy was seen by Waverley of *The Sunday Mail* watching, with that other ex-Celt Joe Cassidy, Celtic beat Rangers 5–0 in a performance which amazed and impressed all Scotland.

Why Tommy was not playing for Third Lanark that day is not clear. He may have been injured or suspended but it is far more likely that he was simply not considered, having burned his boats as far as the Third Lanark management was concerned. On 11 April Celtic won the Scottish Cup against Dundee in what would became known as the Patsy Gallacher Cup Final, while Third Lanark went down to Rangers. Even a 4–0 win at Falkirk on 18 April was not enough to save Third Lanark from their first ever relegation.

Gloom thus descended over Cathkin but the mood at Parkhead was upbeat and euphoric. They had now won the Scottish Cup eleven times, once more than Queen's Park, and there now seemed to be a great prospect in the young McGrory. Maley now moved on 12 May for McInally. 'He was pining for Celtic Park, although he would not say this,' said Maley with a twinkle in his eye. 'In fact we knew he was pining for home,' he would say repeatedly. Indeed McInally was homesick and took no persuasion at all to rejoin Celtic. Promises were made about training hard, staying off the drink and working for the club. Never had there been such rejoicing about the return of a prodigal son. The supporters were supremely happy.

To what extent Maley worked on his own here, and to what extent he consulted the directors or men like captain Willie McStay, we are not sure. Certainly everyone seemed happy, and one significant thing about McInally was that he was a cheap buy (about £2,000 it was said) in that Third Lanark had had enough of him and were glad to get him off their payroll. Apart from the story that went around in March about Rangers – and as we have seen, it may or may not have had some foundation – there was a distinct lack of competition for the signature of Tommy McInally. The mid-1920s was a time when rich English teams came to Scotland brandishing chequebooks for the likes of Hughie Gallacher of Airdrie and Alec James and David Morris of Raith Rovers. There was no such rush for McInally. Indeed the transfer fee was not officially disclosed, but it would not have been much. In any case, Maley and Celtic had spent the last five or six years bleating continually about poverty. He could hardly then have justified paying a large fee for a man who had been a proven failure, no matter how much potential he had shown.

The history of Celtic is of course rich in those who can play only for Celtic and whose attempts to play elsewhere are less successful than when in the green and white. In recent years we can think of Charlie Nicholas and Shaun Maloney. The atmosphere at Celtic Park on matchdays is indeed something special for those who have been brought up on it. It has always been so. Perhaps this was what Tommy McInally was missing. Perhaps in this sense he was indeed 'pining for home'.

Be that as it may, *The Glasgow Herald* on Wednesday 13 May 1925 reported laconically and unspectacularly, 'Celtic FC made a bid for the services of their old centre forward Tom McInally who was with Third Lanark and were successful in securing his transfer at a late hour last night. Aberdeen were also bidding for the player.'

If Tommy had been 'pining for home', he had now been granted his wish.

5

The Glorious Return

Thus it was that the summer of 1925 was spent by Celtic fans in a rare mood of euphoria, tinged with pleasurable anticipation of what was to come. The bad days had now gone, it was felt, and the 5–0 thrashing of Rangers in the Scottish Cup semi final was already much celebrated in song. There is a sad tendency for Celtic supporters to associate 'Hello! Hello!' with Rangers. This is unfortunate for it was originally an American Civil War song called 'Marching Through Georgia' about freeing slaves and when the song came to Scotland Celtic had it first and tied it to the famous Scottish Cup victory masterminded by the inimitable Patsy Gallacher.

> Hello! Hello! We Are The Timalloys
> Hello! Hello! You'll Know Us By The Noise
> We Beat The Rangers In The Cup
> Twas Great To Be Alive
> Not One, Not Two, Not Three Not Four, But Five!

It would continue to be sung about for the next three or four decades. In truth, that game rocked Rangers and they would take some time to recover. The Scottish Cup final against Dundee had shown that Patsy Gallacher was apparently not finished yet (in fact his Parkhead career was all but over, but no-one knew it at that point) and that in the young McGrory who had been given the Scottish Cup to hold by Maley on the bus returning from Hampden that night, Celtic had a fine goalscorer. 'Give young McGrory the Cup,' said Maley. Peter Wilson and Alec Thomson had also won their spurs, but now, to crown it all, the 'boy wonder' was returning – Tommy McInally.

The ancient Greek historian Thucydides, writing the Peloponnesian War of 431 to 404 BC, tells the story of the brilliant but unstable Alcibiades who had deserted Athens for Sparta after being charged with mocking religious practices and defaming statues of Gods. But he repented, and the Athenian government invited him back. He was indeed homesick and 'pining for home'. In 407 BC Xenophon, another historian, described the scene at the harbour as he arrived back where a huge crowd had gathered and he was given a hero's welcome. The past was to be forgotten and everyone was happy that he was back where he belonged. McInally was Celtic's Alcibiades.

Or there is the story of the Prodigal Son in the Gospel according to St. Luke 15 20–24:

And when he was yet a great way off, his father saw him and had compassion and ran and fell on his neck and kissed him. And the son said unto him, 'Father I have sinned against heaven and in thy sight and am no more worthy to be called thy son'. But the Father said to his servants, 'Bring forth the best robe and put it on him; and put a ring on his hand, and shoes on his feet, and bring hither the fatted calf and kill it, and let us eat and be merry, for this my son was dead, and is alive again, he was lost and is found.' And they began to be merry . . .

The parallel is even more striking when one considers the Biblical sequel, for the loyal son who had stayed at home all the time is angry that the prodigal son is now being treated so well, but the Father then says to him, 'Son, thou art ever with me, and all that I have is thine . . . thy brother was dead, and is alive again; and was lost and is found.' If this story was read in church at any time in the summer of 1925, it would have been difficult for Celtic supporters not to equate the prodigal son with McInally, the father with Maley and the dutiful son with Patsy Gallacher.

To what extent Maley bought back (at minimum cost, or perhaps no cost at all if some reports are to be believed) McInally in a deliberate decision to replace Patsy Gallacher is open to question. In practice, this was indeed what happened, but had Maley already made up his mind that it was time for Patsy to move on? Did he know that Patsy had serious injury problems? Or did he feel that it might be an idea to try to play both Gallacher and McInally at the same time? He had of course done this before, and it hadn't been a total success. The truth probably had little to do with Gallacher. Maley knew, as did the rest of the world, that McInally was available and would jump at the chance to play again for his beloved Celtic.

More prosaically, the summer of 1925 also saw a change in the laws of the game. For some time legislators had been concerned about the lack of goals being scored and, feeling that the offside law was partly responsible, now declared that only two defenders needed to be closer to the goal line to ensure that a player was onside, instead of three. This seemed to work to Celtic's advantage for they had always been an attacking free-scoring team and the first game of the season saw them put Hibs to the sword 5–0. McInally, now at inside left, for he could hardly have expected to replace McGrory (he had been equally happy in either position with Third Lanark), did not score but masterminded the attack, exploiting the new offside law with visionary passing and brilliant ball control before a Celtic Park crowd in an overdrive of ecstasy.

In truth, there was a great deal to be happy about in the first few weeks of the season, for the other member of the inside trio, Alec Thomson ('Eckie Tamson' as he was known) from Buckhaven in Fife was also in fine form, feeding off the sustained competence of the half back line of Wilson, McStay and McFarlane and the brilliance of McInally. McInally was now a little heavier than in his first incarnation with the club, and consequently a little slower, but the craft was there, as was the desire to please his public. There was also the streak of rebelliousness but this was confined to meaningless things like wearing his jersey outside his pants, just to be different from everyone else. Maley may well have disapproved, but simply shrugged his shoulders and said, 'That's Tommy!'

James Handley in *The Celtic Story* was impressed by the first few appearances of the second coming of McInally.

McInally had developed into a crafty tactician of the McMenemy type, and with McLean and McFarlane he was to form a polished scheming trio. His exasperating trick of stopping the ball and gazing round him was done with such cool deliberation that everybody else stood and looked on in amazement.

As yet there had been no sight of Patsy Gallacher, but the question was asked: 'Did Celtic need him?' Apart from a strange defeat to an incredulous Dundee United then in their first season in Division One at the primitive Tannadice Park, the form of the team remained good – until one eventful week in early October when Maley made the mistake of bringing back the blatantly half-fit Patsy Gallacher. Patsy had not featured in the early fixtures that season and the team had not really needed him. He had been suspended by the SFA for last season's indiscretions, developed whooping cough, then struggled with his knee. He was in any case now thirty-four.

It was therefore a surprise when Patsy Gallacher was played on the right wing against Airdrie at Broomfield on 3 October. This was a fine Airdrie team with Hughie Gallacher and McInally's friend from Barrhead, Bob McPhail, in the forward line, but even so the 5–1 score line for Airdrie was a shock of seismic proportions. McInally was clearly unhappy at the introduction of Gallacher and gave every impression of sulking, particularly as the team were three down at half time and lost another two goals early in the second half. Celtic's late goal from McGrory is reported as having been greeted with total silence, for the Celtic supporters had gone home.

It was simply 'a bad day at the office' but Maley reacted badly to it. He dropped the wrong person. He seemed to have decided to teach McInally a lesson, but in so doing taught himself a bigger one and lost the Glasgow Cup. He dropped McInally for the Glasgow Cup semi final replay against Rangers, moved Alec Thomson, a right-sided player, to inside left to allow Gallacher back to his inside right position and restored Paddy Connolly to the right wing. This formation had of course been the one that won last year's Scottish Cup, but it had also been less of a success in most games of last season's Scottish League.

It seemed to work, however, for after a 0–0 draw on Tuesday, the same team beat Rangers 2–0 in extra time in the third game on Thursday. In truth, this was a poor Rangers team bereft of their left wing pairing of Tommy Cairns and Alan Morton and still suffering from a Celtic complex caused by the 5–0 demolition in March, but Celtic fans quite rightly saw this as a great victory.

The final of the Glasgow Cup was to be played two days later at Parkhead against Clyde, then in the Second Division. A crowd of 30,000 turned up to see the slaughter of the innocents and Maley made the fatal mistake of retaining Patsy Gallacher, clearly unfit and being asked to play his fourth game in a week, at inside right and keeping, to the exclusion of McInally, Alec Thomson in the inside left position when he seemed happier at inside right. Gallacher struggled with his injury and Celtic paid the penalty for Maley's folly by losing 1–2.

This was the second time that McInally had been out

of the side and the side had suffered. Those with long memories recalled Celtic's defeat by Rangers in the Scottish Cup of March 1920. Maley himself was aware of this, as he lapsed into his brooding melancholia ('he always painted the losers' dressing room with his own particular coat of miserable paint') and perhaps in future he would over-compensate by playing McInally on occasions when he shouldn't have.

Patsy Gallacher's Parkhead career was now at an end, although he would go on to play for Falkirk. He remained on the books for some time, however, and slowly fizzled out. McInally was reinstated and, for the rest of that season, the forward line of Connolly, Thomson, McGrory, McInally and McLean was seldom tinkered with. Bad results were few. Rangers did beat them 1–0 in late October, but Rangers' form against other teams was inconsistent and dismal. Airdrie in fact provided the main challenge for Celtic but the week before Christmas McInally engineered their downfall in a 3–2 win at Parkhead. Hearts and Falkirk also had their moments but Celtic always stayed ahead in the league race.

For Celtic throughout this excellent season, McInally and Thomson were first-rate 'fetch and carry men' for the goalscoring machine that was James Edward McGrory. 'Tireless, tricky, mazy runs, swinging passes'; 'McInally had no equal for doing the right thing at the right time'; 'How glad Mr. Maley will be that Tommy McInally is back in the fold!' were among the press comments as the fans, poverty or no poverty, came back to see Celtic.

On two occasions Tynecastle was the scene of serious

crowd problems caused by crushing rather than any disorder. Twenty February 1926 brought Celtic to Edinburgh in the Scottish Cup and attracted a crowd of 50,500 – far too many for Tynecastle. On several occasions the crowd threatened to spill over and stop the game, and would have done so but for the presence of mounted police who cleared the touchlines at the cost of several minor injuries. McInally, clearly revelling in the huge crowd, scored twice himself and fed McGrory and Connolly for the other two in Celtic's 4–0 win.

The other occasion that Tynecastle saw a huge crowd and a rampant McInally was the semi final a month after the Hearts game. By this time Tommy was a Scottish internationalist having been in the side that beat Ireland at Ibrox at the end of February. In this semi final, Tommy scored first, then after the black and golds of Aberdeen had equalised with a dubious penalty, McInally fed McGrory to score the winner. Aberdeen would insist that McInally handled but the referee was the world famous Tom Dougray of Bellshill with whom no-one argued successfully!

Tommy (as he would do virtually all his life) still lived in Barrhead and Bob McPhail, himself now well established with Airdrieonians, recalled how he frequently shared a railway compartment with Tommy, Peter Wilson of Celtic, Johnny Johnstone of Hearts and Jimmy Maxton, the somewhat controversial Independent Labour Party MP who was once imprisoned during the Great War for his opposition to it. Maxton was also famously suspended in 1923 from the House of Commons for calling Conservative MP Sir Frederick Banbury, who wanted to cut free school milk, a 'murderer'. The short train journey was always an entertaining one with McInally forever arguing good naturedly with the erudite Maxton about politics, and Irish politics in particular, one presumes.

McInally had met Maxton frequently in his brother's shop. Frank McInally was a tobacconist. The cadaverous, unhealthy-looking Maxton was a chain smoker and frequented that shop. Maxton gave no impression of being interested in football, although he was on good terms with Maley and other Celtic characters. His constituency was Bridgeton, not far from Parkhead, and a feature of his constituency life was his personality clashes with the notorious Billy Fullerton, the leader of the odious Orange gangs who called themselves the 'Billy Boys' and whom Maxton despised for they divided the working class.

Some of McPhail's stories about McInally are interesting, such as the time that he was being threatened by a brutal centre half who said to Tommy, 'I'll eat you! Tommy replied, 'Well at least that will get some football into you!' McPhail also stated that, whatever McInally's other vices were, he never swore, and that if he ever heard any foul mouth, even in his own dressing room, he would likely turn, wag his finger and say to the perpetrator, 'You'll go to the big bad fire, son!' McPhail was a wheen less charitable in his opinions of other Celtic players, notably Patsy Gallacher and Willie Cook.

McInally was the perpetual talk of the country that spring of 1926 as Celtic progressed, apparently inexorably, to their double of league and cup. His goals were legendary. Some of them were esoteric and bizarre, but more devastating were the goals that he scored frequently by feinting to pass to the lurking McGrory, drawing a defender or two towards McGrory, then running on to score himself. His dribbling, passing, running and shooting were of the highest order, and the perpetual adulation was by no means undeserved.

The authoritative *The Glory And The Dream*, written by Pat Woods and Tom Campbell, states,

> His (McInally's) control and nerve was such that he could still cause bewilderment among defenders and amusement on the terracings with his patented mannerism of stopping suddenly, in order to look around with casual insolence, before re-directing the flow of the game.

If it was Willie Maley who put the 'tic' in Celtic in the business and political sense, it was certainly McInally who made the team tick on the field and he was the man who brought the crowds in, persuading supporters to pay their money, even in the most desperate of economic circumstances.

Singing was always a great part of football crowds, more so perhaps in the 1920s than in later decades, and many a veteran would lament the passing at Celtic Park of community singing of all the old favourites, including a few already referred to about Tommy McInally. But chanting was something a great deal less common until the 1960s when 'Celtic! Cha! Cha! Cha!' or 'Celtic!' followed by three hand claps became commonplace. There was however one very rhythmical chant about Tommy McInally. It was repetitive and simple to learn but very effective when the ground was full. It went quite simply:

Tommy McInally, Tommy, Tommy, Tommy Mack!
Tommy Tommy Tommy Tommy McInally
Tommy, Tommy Mack!

It was heard frequently that 1925/26 season, for there was much to be happy about in the play of the beloved 'Tommy Mack'.

But the free moving and free scoring forward line had suffered a blow in mid March when Adam McLean had been injured while playing for the Scottish League against the English League. A few bad results (goalless draws in particular) began to creep in to the otherwise excellent form of the team, but no-one could have predicted the cataclysmic loss of the Scottish Cup to St. Mirren in the final on 10 April. A crowd of 98,620 saw a most un-Celtic-like performance. In the first place, they were not wearing the green and white hoops (or stripes as they were called in the 1920s) but came out unaccountably in white. Goalkeeper Peter Shevlin made two uncharacteristic mistakes in the first half hour, and Celtic never fought back as their fans demanded. They did claim that a header from McGrory crossed the line, and they did miss Adam McLean for whom Willie Leitch was a hard working but uninspired replacement, but it was not to be Celtic or Tommy's day.

The downcast McInally admitted that he was poor, that the team never settled and that Celtic were mere shadows of themselves. While it has to be admitted that the Paisley men played above themselves, many Celtic fans were left asking a few questions about this game. Curiously enough, exactly thirty years later in 1956, Celtic underperformed in a Scottish Cup final against

Hearts in similarly puzzling circumstances and on both occasions stories of match-fixing and relationships with bookmakers were not excluded as being too fanciful.

A crumb of comfort was gleaned in the evening papers that night in the news that Cowdenbeath had beaten Airdrie 1–0 and that one point was all that was required for the league championship. Celtic duly achieved that target but in circumstances of anti-climax on a dismal Wednesday afternoon at Parkhead as only 3,000 were there to see McGrory, Connolly and McInally score the goals that beat Morton 3–1. In 1926 the Scottish League Championship was very welcome, and it was McInally's first ever Scottish medal, but the Scottish Cup was far more important and prestigious!

There was in any case no time to bask in any glory for winning the League Championship or self-pity for losing the Scottish Cup. Storm clouds were gathering on the industrial front in the shape of the General Strike, the biggest threat to British capitalism since the Industrial Revolution. The parallel with Russia in 1917 terrified the ruling class, the Royal Family and the Church to an extent that had never been seen before. Spurred on by the miners, the Trade Union Congress was able to grind the wheels of industry to a halt for almost a fortnight before mysteriously giving in. Incredibly, football in the shape of the Glasgow Charity Cup continued during the strike in spite of there being virtually no transport. As all the games were in Glasgow, however, this presented fewer problems than might have been expected.

Celtic redeemed themselves for their Scottish Cup and Glasgow Cup failures by winning the Charity Cup, defeating, on successive Saturdays, Partick Thistle, Third Lanark and then Queen's Park. The final against Queen's Park took place at Ibrox the day after the strike collapsed. In an atmosphere of class hatred with Celtic the archetypal working class team against snooty middle class Queen's Park (several of whose players had broken the strike by driving buses and trains), McInally scored direct from a corner kick (according to some reports, while others say 'resultant from a corner kick') and laid on the winner for McGrory in a 2–1 win which was more emphatic than it sounded. It was, for more reasons than one, particularly sweet for the Parkhead faithful in the 24,000 crowd as strains of 'The Red Flag' resounded round Ibrox, incongruously mingled with 'Erin's Green Valleys'.

The teams were:

Celtic: Shevlin, W. McStay and Callaghan; Wilson, J. McStay and McFarlane; Connolly, Thomson, McGrory, McInally and McLean

Queen's Park: Harkness, Barrie and Wiseman; Langmuir, Gillespie and Moreland; Crawford, Russell, McDonald, McAlpine and Nicholson

Thus ended McInally's first season in his second spell with the club. It had been a good one. The plus points had been the winning of the Scottish League and the Glasgow Charity Cup, some beautiful football and exquisite goals and his first international cap. The debits had been the loss of the two other trophies in heartrending circumstances at the final stage – the Glasgow Cup being particularly galling, for Tommy had been unfairly dropped and the Scottish Cup remaining the one major blot on the landscape in 1926 – and his own personal disappointment at not retaining his Scotland place for the 'big' international against England at Old Trafford after he had played well against Ireland.

But he was very much in credit. Willie Maley was certainly in no doubt: 'I am sure I will be pardoned in giving Tommy McInally a special pat for his wonderful work as leader and mentor to our young forwards, a position which, I hope, he will be long spared to fill.' The Celtic fans concurred with their leader's assessment of their prize asset. McInally was as popular with the Celtic fans as he had been in his glorious first season in 1919/20.

In 1926 Celtic fans needed something to cheer them up. The aftermath of the General Strike (the miners continued their own strike until the autumn) saw a continuation of the dreadful poverty that had befouled Scotland since the Industrial Revolution of more than 100 years previously. Old timers still smile patronisingly as the modern media screeches about 'credit crunch', 'falling house prices' and 'recession'. The poverty of the 1920s resembled that of the Third World under a government of Stanley Baldwin and Winston Churchill in no way sympathetic to the working class. There had in 1924 been the brief Labour government of Ramsay MacDonald, but it had been a minority one and had not lasted more than a few months. The Welfare State was still a couple of decades and another world war away in the future.

In these circumstances, people needed their social life, their leisure activities and their heroes. Dancing was a great Glaswegian social activity, as was going to the cinema. The football season of 1926/27 was just starting when the news broke that the great cinema hero Rudolf Valentino had died. Women everywhere were devastated – from Pola Negri, the actress who had a bad attack of 'the vapours' and pronounced herself 'ill with grief', to the working class women of the Glasgow slums who had always hoped that Valentino would come and rescue them from drunken husbands and relentless poverty. Harry Houdini, the escapologist, would die soon too. It was just as well that Glasgow retained its clown prince – Tommy McInally.

But another Celtic hero was on his way to pastures new. Patsy Gallacher had hardly played last season, and when he had, it had been to the team's detriment. Eventually, after prolonged and undignified wrangling, Patsy departed for Falkirk on 1 October 1926. Yet another Celtic hero, the great Joe Cassidy, made no bones about the fact that he wanted back to Celtic (like McInally, he too was 'pining for home') but settled for Dundee where Alec McNair was the manager.

In truth, the league winning team of Shevlin, W. McStay and Hilley; Wilson, J. McStay and McFarlane; Connolly, Thomson, McGrory, McInally and McLean looked at the start of the season capable of doing it again. Although McInally was out with an injury in September, he was back for the Glasgow Cup which Celtic won on 9 October. It was McInally's third Glasgow Cup medal, this time won in a gale at Hampden as they beat Rangers 1–0. Fifty-one thousand attended this game and it all hinged on a McInally pass to McGrory. Rangers had benefitted from the west-to-east gale (some say 'hurricane') in the first half, but the Celtic defence, with John Donoghue deputising for the injured Jimmy McStay, had been resolute. Then, in the second half, Celtic took over and really should have scored more than the one that they got.

The teams were:

Celtic: Shevlin, W. McStay and Hilley; Wilson, Donoghue and McFarlane; Connolly, Thomson, McGrory, McInally and McLean

Rangers: Hamilton, Purdon and McCandless; Craig, Shaw and Muirhead; Archibald, McKay, Henderson, Cunningham and Fleming

At this point McInally was very clearly toeing the line and reaping the benefit. He earned his second Scotland cap at the end of October (and Scotland won again) and his form for Celtic was consistently good, although it is fair to say that it was the goal scoring exploits of Jimmy McGrory which caught the eye. On three occasions that season McGrory scored five in a game (on one such day against Aberdeen at Parkhead on 23 October 1926, four of them were scored with his head!) and several other times he hit four. He totalled fifty-nine that season – and missed the last five league matches and the Scottish Cup final through injury!

The modest McGrory would always pay credit to the rest of his forward line. There was Paddy Connolly, a right winger well worth a mention among Celtic's great right wingers like Jimmy Delaney and Jimmy Johnstone; there was Mr Ever-Ready, 'McGrory's fetch and carry man', the perpetual supplier of the ammunition in the tireless, toothless Alec Thomson; there was the quiet, unflamboyant, business-like Adam McLean, who would have won far more Scotland caps had he not arrived at the same time as Alan Morton and Alec Troup; and there was, of course, the perpetual court jester, the man who could be guaranteed to put a smile on any face, the Cinquevalli of the football field, in Tommy McInally. 'Snally', as he was nicknamed, remained the darling of the Celtic Park terraces – at least for the time being.

He was rumoured to be not the most enthusiastic of trainers, and he did keep company with a few seedy characters, and as McGrory would put it in a gentlemanly meiosis, 'Tommy was not averse to a tipple', but in the eyes of Tommy's fans, this made him even more popular. He was even more 'one of us', and Tommy never tried to be anything else. He loved the fans, they loved him, everyone loved 'the Cellic', and as long as things were going well on the field, as they clearly were in late 1926, there was no problem with Tommy McInally.

Manager Maley indulged Tommy too. Maley, strict and firm on the outside, had managed more than his fair share of bad boys in the past. He had seen Dan Doyle and Patsy Gallacher, for instance, not to mention many of lesser ability like Johnny Browning and Mick McKeown, and he was learning how to deal with McInally, or so he thought. This included developing a sense of humour. One day he upbraided Tommy for having been seen coming out of a public house at 9.30pm. 'Aye, boss,' replied Tommy, 'I had tae come oot then. They were closin'!' Maley was forced to smile. It was basically a good relationship between Maley and McInally.

Yet, as any teacher of a bad boy will know, there is seldom a total reformation, seldom is there a Road to Damascus moment when everything suddenly undergoes a revolutionary change. The transformation behind such words and phrases as 'turning the corner' and 'turning over a new leaf' tends to be a gradual process. There are usually moments of backsliding – and sometimes a total reversal to the bad old ways.

New Year 1927 saw a downturn in Celtic's fortunes. The Old Firm game was played at Ibrox, again in a gale, but this time it was Celtic who were unlucky as Rangers edged a late winner after the teams had been locked at 1–1. As has often happened in Celtic's history, they allowed themselves to be upset by this unlucky reverse and promptly lost their next game to Queen's Park at Parkhead. A great deal of this was caused by playing a half-fit Jimmy McStay at centre half, but it was a bad New Year and one which would cost Celtic dear in the race for the championship.

The Scottish Cup got off to a poor start at Dumfries where, in a 0–0 draw on 22 January, McInally seemed to have been the only player to have pulled his weight. *The Glasgow Observer* reported that 'McInally was the dominating personality afield. Tommy worked the full ninety minutes'. He was then outstanding in the replay on Wednesday afternoon when Celtic won 4–1. The game was played in a heavy storm and at one point a chunk of the Grant Stand blew off into the crowd. This would have ramifications, for Celtic now decided that a new stand would need to be built. Money would be required for this and players would have to be sold.

February saw momentous happenings at Brechin. Celtic were drawn there in the Scottish Cup. The Angus farmer by the name of Wattie Gentles did not realise what he was starting. He scored first for Brechin City and went on to score a hat-trick. Fortunately for Celtic, McInally and McGrory were able to organise the rescue and Celtic won 6–3, but Maley now decided that enough was enough for goalkeeper Peter Shevlin, who had been partly blamed for some of the goals lost at the New Year too, not to mention his horrendous performance in the previous year's Scottish Cup final. Peter was dropped and in came a young lad from Fife by the name of John Thomson.

John was shy, overawed and not a little afraid of the streetwise McInally. He needn't have been. Tommy had been shy himself once (although in all honesty he hid it better) and made young Thomson welcome, seeing at once that there was real quality in this young boy. In fact John already knew his namesake, Alec, with whom he had played for the same Fife junior team, Wellesley Juniors. John now played for the rest of the season, impressing everyone with his agility and confidence.

Celtic's Scottish Cup campaign continued with a good win at Dundee, with 'McInally doing all the forcing' (on the day when the 'woefully weak' Joe Cassidy, now playing for Dundee, had the negro slave song 'Poor Old Joe' sung to him) then the club's first ever visit to Newtown Park, Bo'ness to meet the leaders of the Second Division, whom they beat 5–2. But, as often happens when the team are going well in the Scottish Cup (which was, after all, considered to be the more important trophy in the 1920s), league form slumped and, as several players temporarily lost form, Celtic drew at Pittodrie on a Wednesday afternoon then lost at Cowdenbeath in an unpleasant game before the league challenge finally evaporated with a 0–3 defeat at Hearts in a game on 30 March where McInally was carried off with a broken nose.

By this time, however, Celtic were in the Scottish Cup final. This had been achieved by a 1–0 win over Falkirk at Ibrox in the semi final on 26 March. Falkirk, of course, contained Patsy Gallacher and this was the famous game in which the Celtic fans sang 'Will you no' come back again?' for their hero. McInally, of course, emphatically did *not* want Patsy to come back again, and set out that day to prove that he, and no-one else, was now the shining star in the Celtic Park pantheon. It was no easy task, for Patsy could still produce the goods (it had been Patsy who had beaten Rangers in the previous round for Falkirk) and set out to take on McInally in a few jousts to prove a point. Sadly for Patsy, he came off second best. McInally was the best player on the pitch and set up Adam McLean for the only goal of the game.

Celtic were surprised to hear that their opponents in the Scottish Cup final of 16 April 1927 would be East Fife, who had delighted and surprised their supporters and the rest of Scotland by beating Partick Thistle 2–1 in the other semi final at Tynecastle. East Fife, from a community still devastated by the General Strike and the Miners Strike, which lasted until autumn 1926, were in the Second Division and were the first team ever from a lower division to reach the final. It was widely expected, however, that Celtic would beat them. Indeed, they were firm favourites.

Tommy's broken nose healed in time for the final but an equally serious blow had been dealt to Celtic in a nasty league game at Falkirk on Wednesday 6 April when Jimmy McGrory was carried off with two broken ribs. Falkirk had a point to prove about their semi final defeat, Patsy Gallacher still had an axe to grind – and this time no McInally to oppose him, for McInally was sitting in the stand with his nose in plaster – and the whole thing had been made a lot worse by events the previous Saturday.

Scotland had lost to England at Hampden – a very rare phenomenon in the 1920s and, indeed, Scotland's first ever defeat at the New Hampden since it was built in 1903. Gloom had spread throughout the whole nation in a way that really only happens in a military defeat in a war. McInally milked the situation by talking through his broken nose, exaggerating and talking as if he had a harelip, and saying that Scotland would have won if he had been playing. But Willie McStay had really stirred it up by saying that Robert Thomson of Falkirk was the cause of the defeat. 'If Hilley or Hutton had partnered me instead of Thomson, Scotland would not have lost.'

This created a somewhat poisonous atmosphere at Brockville. A less tolerant referee might have sent off a few from each side for the many crunching tackles on the hard pitch. The result, a 1–4 defeat, did not matter much, for the league was almost certainly lost anyway. More important was the injury to McGrory. McInally realised that McGrory was out for the final and that in all probability this would mean that he would be asked to return to his original role as centre forward for the big game. He must therefore be fit.

He did play in a game at Tannadice Park which, although it was a fatal nail in Dundee United's coffin for they would be relegated that year, was meaningless for Celtic and he scored in the 3–3 draw. At one point he appealed for a penalty and *The Sporting Post* asked, 'Doesn't Tommy do a tremendous lot of appealing in the course of an afternoon?' He was desperate to play in the Scottish Cup final, and it was just as well that he did, for history now remembers this as the Tommy McInally Cup Final.

It could also be termed 'the Wireless Cup Final', for it was the first Scottish Cup final to be broadcast live. This new medium of communication had been gaining ground throughout the 1920s and the BBC was now in existence. The first radio station in Scotland had opened on 6 March 1923. A few none-too-successful attempts had been made to broadcast football games in the early months of 1927, but then in early April the Scotland v England game was put on the nation's airwaves. Ownership of these expensive sets, which required either an electricity connection or what was known as a 'battery accumulator', was limited to only a few eccentrics and those who had a great deal of money, but as word spread quickly that one heard 'every single word' from the Hampden international and that Scottish country dance music could also be heard in the evening, a mini boom in radios became apparent and the BBC announced that it would 'attempt to broadcast' a 'running commentary of the final tie of the Scottish Association Cup'.

Here, some enterprise was shown as well. In Methil, home of East Fife, the Oriental Soda Bar in the High Street announced that the game would be 'broadcasted' *(sic)* for the benefit of its customers. This had been done with tolerable success in the international and would be done again for the English Cup final between Cardiff City and Arsenal the following week. This was the 1920s prototype of 'going to the pub to watch Sky', and the following week the proprietors were glad to announce that business had been 'brisker than normal'.

For Celtic the absence of McGrory meant the deployment of McInally (now twelve stones in weight according to some newspapers on the morning of the game) in his original position of centre forward and the drafting in of young John McMenemy, the son of the great 'Napoleon' with whom Tommy had played a few games in the 1919/20 season. Young John McMenemy (who had only played two games previously for the club) and the other John, Thomson, were shaking with nerves, and had to be upbraided by Maley. They were given a pompous homily about it being an 'honour and a privilege to play for the green and white jerseys', that 'it should be the opposition who should be shaking' and to 'get out and bring me back that Cup'. This frankly had not helped, but what did settle everyone was when Maley left and Tommy McInally took over the dressing room with his jokes, banter and clowning, achieving, it was said, the remarkable feat of telling a string of dirty jokes without ever using a bad word. For Tommy, remember, did not swear. He may have been proficient in most of the other deadly sins, but a foul mouth was not his problem.

The phrase 'get out and bring me back that Cup' had also been used by Maley a few days previously when captain Willie McStay, egged on by McInally, had approached Maley to ask if there was to be a special bonus for beating East Fife to win the Scottish Cup. Now Maley did not like that sort of thing and it was only a few years earlier that Willie Cringan had been shown the door for daring to make such a request. So McStay took McInally in with him, knowing that Maley would not lose his temper at his beloved prodigy. This was sound reasoning, but Maley was obdurate, and the answer was: 'No. You want a special bonus for beating a team of miners from Fife? A second division team! Part timers! Third raters! Get out and bring me back that Cup!'

A crowd of 80,070 were at Hampden that pleasant spring Saturday of 16 April 1927, to see the following teams take the field:

Celtic: J. Thomson, W. McStay and Hilley; Wilson,
J. McStay and McFarlane; Connolly,
A. Thomson, McInally, McMenemy and
McLean.

East Fife: Gilfillan, Robertson and Gillespie; Hope,
Brown and Russell; Weir, Paterson, Wood,
Barrett and Edgar.

East Fife, who had already beaten Aberdeen and Partick Thistle to reach the final, shocked everyone by scoring first. Jock Wood headed home an Edgar cross in seven minutes to what was described in some papers (perhaps a little tastelessly) as a 'titanic roar of delight' from the Fife fans and the neutrals who wished to see an even game. Sadly for East Fife, a minute later an own goal restored the balance, and after that McInally took command.

Adam McLean scored before half time and Paddy Connolly immediately after, and the game ended long before referee Tom Dougray from Bellshill blew the final whistle. McInally clowned and capered endlessly, earning plaudits from his adoring fans who knew that the cup was going to be won for the twelfth time. He did impersonations of the famous Charlie Chaplin walk, he dribbled with the ball, played keepy-uppy with it and retained possession of it, always being able to dodge the strong tackles of defenders, as the 'green and white supporters began to chant their weird ditties that seem to be dear to their hearts. The bigger the leads, the more mournful the dirge,' said *The Sporting Post*.

McInally made no attempt to score, for he did not want to humiliate the Second Division Fifers who might easily have conceded ten goals that day, such was the power of Celtic. McInally even deliberately missed a few by hitting them high into the crowd. The following day *The Sunday Mail* reported,

McInally delighted the now happy Celtic choristers with a few of the balloon variety . . . And some of Tommy's late tries added to the merriment of the bulk of the

80,000 crowd who had by this time ceased to regard what they were seeing as a contest . . . How they did laugh as Tommy sent high over the top a sweet thing (sic) which McLean 'left on' for him a minute or so before the final whistle.

The Leven Mail, the newspaper of the losers, was less impressed. While agreeing that Celtic were a cut above the gallant East Fife who came back, however, from Hampden 'not without a great deal of credit and glory', and admitting that McInally 'distributed well' in the centre forward position, the writer then said that 'McInally should have been banished for the chances he missed', clearly failing to catch the mood of the occasion. No doubt, he would have enjoyed telling his readers how East Fife were the first team to have conceded a Scottish Cup final to a double figure scoreline, if indeed McInally had taken all his chances.

It was Tommy's finest hour – a combination of his beloved team winning the Scottish Cup and of himself being the centre of attention. At full time he made a point of shaking hands with the referee, every one of the East Fife players and even a few members of the crowd. The cup was of course presented in those days to the directors of the club in the Hampden board room, but every member of that crowd left Hampden convinced that this was the Tommy McInally show. Maley, it was said, mildly rebuked McInally for not scoring more goals, but Tommy replied, 'Ach, boss, I didnae want tae score mair goals that Jimmy McGrory. I'm well past being another McGrory.'

It did not seem to matter that the rest of the season was spent with Tommy playing at half pace. Two defeats from Rangers (one in the league the Monday after the Scottish Cup Final and the other in the Glasgow Charity Cup) caused little concern, even though it was plain that Tommy was not bothering, now that he had won his Scottish Cup medal. Perhaps he was miffed at not being invited to tour Canada with the SFA party along with Willie McStay, Jimmy McStay, Adam McLean and Patsy Gallacher (who was not even Scottish!), but, for whatever reason, Tommy was simply not in top gear or anything like it and Celtic therefore suffered. Maley, still basking in the Scottish Cup triumph, was slow in recognising the signs here. Had he taken action earlier and more strongly, the next season, a disastrous one with long-term implications, might not have happened.

Tommy did, however, suffer a family bereavement in the death of his older brother Francis who had been ill for some time with pernicious anaemia, and who died in May, unmarried aged forty-seven, at the family home of 28 Carlibar Road, Barrhead. Francis, the tobacconist and commonly known as Frank, was some twenty years older than Tommy, and may have been the closest thing to a father that Tommy had. One wonders whether the loss of Francis played a big part in Tommy going off the rails in season 1927/28.

But Tommy remained, for the moment, irrepressible. A couple of months later, at the Glasgow Police Sports five-a-side at Ibrox, Tommy almost caused a riot by refusing to get off the ball which he sat upon and incited the Partick Thistle players, Willie Salisbury in particular, to get it from him. Some reports deny that he actually sat on the ball, claiming that he only stood with

Tommy's brother Arthur is third from the left at the back of this school photograph taken during the Great War. The boy standing on the extreme right is possibly Tommy

"The Boy Wonder". Tommy is sitting down on the extreme right of this picture taken at the start of the 1919/20 season

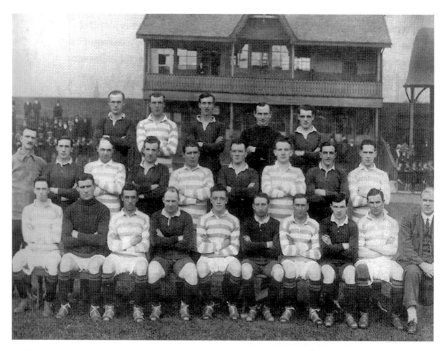

Celtic at the start of the 1921/22 season. Tommy is in the middle row third from the right. Behind is the famous pavilion in the north-west corner of the ground

Tommy in one of Celtic's change strips of green with a white V

Celtic's famous forward line of the mid-1920s with Paddy Connolly, Alec Thomson, Jimmy McGrory, Tommy McInally and Adam McLean. Tommy, rebellious as ever, has his shirt outside his pants!

Tommy in typically relaxed pose (second from left at the back) before a match in Third Lanark's tour of Argentina in 1923. Observe the distinctive collars of Third Lanark

The superb league-winning Celtic team of 1925/26. Tommy the mastermind is second from the left in the back row

Celtic at the start of Tommy's last season for the club with the Glasgow Cup and Scottish Cup in front of them. Tommy is sitting on the extreme left

Team photo from a match between Celtic and Cardiff City (the Cup winners of Scotland and England) in October 1927. Tommy is third from the left in the front row

14 April 1928, the day of the disastrous 0-4 Scottish Cup Final. Tommy (extreme left) watches John Thomson save from Rangers' Jimmy Fleming

7 September 1929, the day of the opening of Sunderland's new stand at Roker Park. Tommy is second from the right in the front row. Next to him is Adam McLean and the bowlerhatted manager is Johnny Cochrane

Tommy's unfortunate headline remark on his departure from Sunderland

"Kept Out by Novices"— McInally

"ARGUS" TELLS ABOUT

THE FREE TRANSFER

RIDDLE : INQUIRIES

ABOUT ANDREWS

A. ANDREWS

4 January 1932, his playing career more or less over. Tommy acted as linesman in Patsy Gallacher's benefit. He is on the extreme left wearing plus fours

"The Boys of the Old Brigade" – a collection of ex-Celts taken sometime in the late 1940s or early 1950s. The fat faced Tommy is third from the right

Tom Higgins, one time Headmaster of St. Cuthbert's High School and great nephew of Tommy McInally on holiday in Prague

This is a picture of Michael McInally, great nephew of Tommy

The Celtic connection! Henrik Larsson is the man on the right, and the policeman is Tom McInally, the great nephew of Tommy

The author with the 2008 SPL trophy

A family portrait of Tommy McInally

his foot on the ball and yawned histrionically. Jimmy McGrory says that Tommy did indeed sit on the ball and adds the detail that he chewed some blades of grass as well. But the Thistle players all hung back, terrified of a humiliation caused by Scotland's No. 1 personality in 1927 – Tommy McInally. This did not go down well with the crowd who had of course come to see football, not McInally clowning, and after laughing a little at the start, the laughs turned to catcalls and boos. Tommy eventually kicked the ball out of play. The Celtic directors were moved to promise that there would be no repetition. Indeed, the last laugh was on Celtic, for Partick Thistle won the game!

It is a mark of Tommy McInally's subsequent persona that this story has grown arms and legs. The fact that it happened at Ibrox has encouraged the belief that it was against Rangers – whereas it was definitely Partick Thistle – and some folk, even John MacAdam, the respected journalist of Charles Buchan's *Football Monthly*, in his tribute to Tommy in March 1956 claimed that 'there was almost a break-in before they got McInally off his roost.' It is a shame when facts get in the way of a good story, but then again, Tommy was the sort of man who would have attracted that sort of exaggeration. Indeed, he himself would have positively encouraged it!

6

Disaster and Departure

Season 1927/28 started with McInally once again irre-pressible, but what struck the observer was the weight that he had put on. Yet the *The Dundee Courier* of early October, a propos Tommy's decisive role in a good 4–1 win at Dens Park ('all the Celts were good – McInally and McGrory extra good') stated that 'Tommy's shadow grows no less but he carries his avoirdupois without seeming difficulty' and that he was as light on his feet as 'an Irish ragman' – an odd simile to our modern ears – and on 8 October he won yet another Glasgow Cup medal as Celtic beat Rangers 2–1. John Thomson was superb but the 'craft of McInally' was once again the centre of attention as he ignored all the cries about his size from the Rangers end of Hampden and delighted the Celtic connoisseurs at the other side.

His weight was particularly noticeable about the knees and it soon became a talking point. When he damaged his ankle, for example, in a game against Raith Rovers in early September and missed the next two games, it was speculated whether his weight might have been a contributory problem in that his ankle was being asked to carry too much! When the circus came to town, there was always the 'Fat Lady'. Was she as fat as Tommy McInally, however, people asked? But it must be recognised that in the 1920s, fatness (or obesity) was not necessarily seen as the problem that it became in the later years of the twentieth century. In those consumptive, under-fed days, the putting on of weight was often seen as a welcome sight. Fatness equalled health.

Catching this mood, the Glaxo Baby Food firm had an advertisement that was seen on all billboards. There was a picture of a fat, red cheeked, smiling baby with the caption underneath that said 'He's glad his mother feeds him Glaxo'. It struck a chord with the population, and very soon Tommy and other fat people began to get the nickname 'the Glaxo Baby'. It was a flattering and a welcome name for most people, but hardly for a professional footballer! He also earned another less than welcome nickname in 'Chocolate Tommy'.

McInally had a reputation for being pugnacious and ready to fight. In the game against Dundee, for example, he and 'Jock' Thomson had a confrontation which fortunately 'did not get past the primitive stage' as *The Sporting Post* put it. 'Still, there was always the danger of the jukes *(sic)* going up there', the 'jukes' being an old Scottish word for 'fists'. Fortunately, Tommy was normally able to control his temper but, at his weight, he would have been a fearsome sight.

On the Monday holiday of 3 October, Celtic arranged a game against Cardiff City, who had won the English Cup in 1927. This was a 1920s prototype of the Cup Winners Cup and Celtic won 4–1. These sort of games were important to Maley, who always saw Celtic in a British dimension, and his star man McInally was on song that day, feeding McGrory liberally for his four goals. Then on the Saturday afterwards at Hampden, before 90,000, McInally won his fourth Glasgow Cup medal when Celtic beat Rangers 2–1 in a tight game.

McInally had to do his fair share of defending and John Thomson was outstanding, but it was McInally's brilliant defence-splitting pass which set up McGrory for the first goal. It was also the first time that he had faced Bob McPhail, his old Barrhead friend, in an Old Firm context. It was then first blood for Celtic in the 1927/28 season and the delighted fans who poured out of Hampden singing the praises of their team and Tommy McInally could hardly have predicted what the rest of the season would bring.

The teams were:

Celtic: Thomson, W. McStay and McGonagle; Wilson, J. McStay and McFarlane; Connolly, Thomson, McGrory, McInally and McLean

Rangers: Hamilton, Gray and McCandless; Meiklejohn, Simpson and Craig; Archibald, Cunningham, Fleming, McPhail and Morton.

Tommy's problems began the week after the Glasgow Cup victory when Rangers gained a little revenge by winning a league game 1–0 at Ibrox. Rangers scored in the first half from what looked to the press, and certainly to the Celtic fans, to be an offside position. McInally made his point to referee Willie Bell and was warned to keep quiet. He didn't, kept on and on about it as the teams left the field at half time and even when they came out again, and eventually in the sixty-first minute, Bell's patience cracked and McInally was sent off, as police were moved in strength to the Celtic end of the ground where a riot threatened.

McInally was suspended for fourteen days (and manager Maley was cautioned for a similar inability to keep quiet), thereby losing what little chance he had of regaining his Scotland place for the game against Wales on 29 October in Cardiff. He hardly helped his cause either by making an 'unpleasant remark' to referee Bell when he met him in the corridor after the hearing held in the SFA Council Chamber on 19 October. Bell reported the remark, but there was no addition to the fourteen days already given. Without McInally, Celtic lost to Aberdeen at Pittodrie.

It was during his enforced leisure that Tommy seems to have gone all to seed. If he did not train adequately for a game when he was playing, he was not likely to keep fit when he wasn't. He did score a hat-trick against Airdrie on his first game back, but November 1927 saw the form of McInally decline, and the performances of the team suffer. A disappointing draw against Hearts (even though it was 'a most interesting match to watch' and Celtic fought back from being 0–2 down) and an insipid share of the points with Cowdenbeath had led supporters and colleagues to question the fitness, and even the commitment, of the man who had been the hero of the hour so recently. Things came to a head in the game on 3 December at Parkhead when Motherwell registered their first ever win at that ground. McInally, although clearly overweight, played and indeed scored Celtic's only goal in the 2–1 defeat. It was a tap-in from a goalkeeping error on the stroke of half time – and even then there was some doubt about it for Motherwell protested vigorously – but it was more or less the only good thing that he did in the whole game.

In the second half, with the score at 1–1, Celtic enjoyed the bulk of the pressure, but the fine work of Peter Wilson and 'Jean' McFarlane came to nothing whenever the ball reached McInally. He shouted for the ball, but could not control it; he was presented with a gilt-edged opportunity, but miskicked; he refused to run for many balls that were well within his compass, and as always happens when things were going wrong, he blamed everyone else, even the eager youngsters Alec Thomson and Jimmy McGrory, who were clearly still in awe of his tremendous aura and persona. Gradually, the Celtic pressure fizzled out, then Motherwell scored a late winner. Full time came with a crescendo of booing as the 20,000 crowd turned on McInally. Tommy was by no means the only disappointment that day, but he was the most obvious and the Celtic crowd were looking for a scapegoat.

Very clearly, idols have feet of clay, but this was more than a temporary fall from grace and the following midweek *The Glasgow Observer*, in tones more of sorrow rather than anger, said, 'McInally was deficient in every phase . . . it is no use trying to walk through a match . . . his stand-and-wait policy cut no ice.' The fans were in no doubt as to what was causing all this. Glasgow being the 'gossipy village' that it could sometimes be rather than the 'Second City of the Empire' as it claimed to be, yielded all sorts of stories about how someone's brother had seen McInally in several pubs for many nights in a row, someone else had seen the police bring him home, only refraining from arresting him simply because of who he was . . .

These stories were not necessarily all true, but they were believed. Maley had to act. Tommy was carpeted and suspended for three weeks and told to get his act together and come back after Christmas. The following Saturday saw Celtic at Perth winning 5–3 without Tommy. Tommy allegedly appeared at Buchanan Street Station as the team were departing, not to give them best wishes but to deliver a volley of ill-tempered abuse (but, still, apparently true to himself in not swearing!) then went to see his local Barrhead team Arthurlie (with whom he had many family connections) beat Morton 4–2 in the Second Division, leading to all sorts of speculation that he was about to be sacked by Celtic and to join Arthurlie instead. Tommy did nothing to discourage this as he, charming as ever, chatted to other spectators and told everyone who was prepared to listen what an old bore Willie Maley was.

This was, however, only half the story. Tommy was aware of his fitness problem and although, under the terms of his club suspension, not allowed to train at Parkhead, he nevertheless began to train on his own. Residents of Barrhead would see a portly, track-suited figure charging round the streets as McInally made an effort to get fitter. In fact, he trained better on his own. In company of others, he could never concentrate or resist the temptation to show off in front of other players by telling jokes.

But he did have one friend who often trained with him. This was Tommy Milligan, British and European middleweight boxing champion from 1926 until 1928. Milligan was born in Edinburgh but spent most of his life in Shieldmuir in Lanarkshire. Celtic daft, Milligan was well known at Celtic Park, like subsequent boxers Bennie Lynch and Pat Clinton, occasionally using the facilities of the gymnasium. The two Tommys, Milligan and McInally, became friends and Milligan, a far more sensitive and restrained man than McInally, would try his best to make sure that McInally did his bit at training. He would be only intermittently successful in that respect however.

The day after Christmas 1927 saw Tommy in Maley's office, full of apologies and contrition, promising to train harder, to lay off the drink and spinning tales about some ill-defined unhappiness in his private life (to do with a woman, perhaps?) which had now however been sorted out, and how 1928, if he was allowed back, would be as good for Celtic and McInally as 1926 and 1927 had been.

Maley's swallowing of pride would have been heard all over Glasgow, but his statesmanship in allowing McInally back seemed to have yielded dividends when, after bad weather put paid to the game against Raith Rovers on Hogmanay, McInally was included in the team which beat Rangers 1–0 at Parkhead on 2 January 1928. Tommy did not star, but he did not flop either. He did, however, look a little slimmer and seemed eager to play, chasing and foraging and on many occasions getting the better of Rangers' now ageing wing half Tommy Muirhead. He was well received also by the

Celtic crowd. It was a reprieve for McInally's Celtic career . . . but only a temporary one.

On 14 January 1928, McInally took part in a truly momentous occasion, albeit only in a supporting role. This was the day that Dunfermline Athletic came to Glasgow, lost 0–9 and Jimmy McGrory broke all records by scoring eight. McGrory, modest as always, attributed much of his success to the service he received from his two inside forwards, Alec Thomson and Tommy McInally, but it was certainly McGrory's day. McInally, genuinely pleased for his friend Jimmy McGrory, nevertheless found it difficult to be only second best in the 'limelight stakes' and, as we have noticed before, would be quite happy to do something to get people to talk about him, even if it was bad – a feature of many bad, disturbed and maladjusted children.

Tommy's first aberration came after a Scottish Cup game at Keith in early February. Celtic's visit to Kynoch Park attracted a great deal of local attention with a record crowd of 5,200 and Maley, very aware that Celtic had many admirers in all parts of Scotland now, was determined to show the best side of Celtic. This was the first time they had been further north than Aberdeen on official business, although they had toured the Highlands to play friendlies before. The team arrived early, Maley encouraged local photographers and journalists to see his players, took a great deal of interest in local life, and generally Celtic came out of this occasion very well. The 6–1 victory was predictable but full of sparkling football as McGrory and McInally shared the goals, three each.

There is a story about this game, perhaps apocryphal,

but certainly credible in the context of McInally's strange behaviour at the previous year's Scottish Cup Final. A local tailor in Keith had offered a free made-to-measure suit for any Keith player who scored a goal against Celtic. Frankly this was not looking likely as the local lads were totally overwhelmed and, with five minutes left, Celtic were 5–0 up and clearly taking their foot off the pedal. McInally suddenly decided that one of these nice chaps deserved a made-to-measure suit, got the ball, started running back into his own half and 'passed' for a bewildered Keith man called Duncan to put the ball past John Thomson! McInally was then the first to congratulate the man on his new suit, saying things like, 'Ah'm sure the lassies'll fancy you in it.' McGrory then scored again at the other end and the game finished 6–1.

To what extent this story is true (the press reports said 'Duncan picked up a loose ball' or 'a misdirected pass gave Duncan an opportunity') we cannot say, but if it is true, then it could give us a clue to explain what happened next. Suddenly, after the game, McInally went missing! No-one knew what had happened. Wild rumours about kidnaps and murders were not discounted by the local police, and the team returned to Glasgow without Tommy McInally. It is possible that he had an argument with his team mates after his bizarre behaviour. Men like the McStay brothers and Peter McGonagle were thorough professionals and hated losing any goal. They would have taken umbrage at McInally, having already had more of him this season than they could take. He also, one imagines, would have been on the wrong end of a rocket from Maley. One story was that at the small Keith station, Tommy joined the train with his team mates and under the eye of Maley, but then just as the train was about to leave, he disappeared out the other side of the train. Again, one must not rush to believe that story either!

In any case McInally disappeared, but before he could become the Lord Lucan of the 1920s, he turned up again a few days later. Celtic, in contrast to their normal 'open' policy with the press, said nothing, but it was noticeable that there was a distinct lack of hysteria from them, as if they knew that all would be well. Whatever was said or done to McInally, it happened in private, and at the end of the week, McInally found himself back in the team, scoring the only goal of the game as Celtic beat Clyde 1–0 at Shawfield.

This was a strange business and the truth never really had been established. There may have been a Highland lady involved but the likelihood is that Tommy was on a 'bender' – the Scottish word for a period of a few days when alcohol takes over. With retrospect, it would have been in everyone's interest – the team, his fellow players and Tommy himself – if Maley at this point had insisted on some serious 'alcohol advice' from an expert followed by a period in 'dry dock', as detoxification was then commonly known. But Maley, having recently seen McInally out of the team, on this occasion, as so often in the past, was tolerant. 'I always had a soft spot for the boy,' he kept saying. On this occasion, the 'soft spot' was misguided.

Following a tolerably successful February, matters came to a head in early March. Fans waking up on the morning of 3 March and relishing the prospect of the

Motherwell v Celtic Scottish Cup quarter final were appalled to get their morning papers with the banner headlines 'McInally Suspended'. Some newspapers added 'again' and others added 'yet again', but there would be no McInally at Fir Park, nor for the next few weeks. Celtic's directors, having made the decision, were careful not to set a limit on the suspension. They wished to give themselves some leeway.

It had all happened at Seamill Hydro, a favourite retreat of Celtic's before big games. As it was a Hydro Hotel with no alcohol sold or served on the premises, Maley could keep an eye on his errant players. The team had been there all week, and on the Thursday night, the phone rang with someone wanting to talk to Mr. McInally. The voice said it was a well-known newspaper, that they were intending to do a feature on Tommy and could they have a few quotes?

McInally, unable to resist a little more exposure, and a substantial fee – indeed he was a great 'mole' as far as the press were concerned – spoke at length until a few giggles gave the game away. It was his team mates 'having him on' from another phone in the hotel. Tommy, himself a great prankster, could not cope with pranks being played on him, and shouting that he had had enough of Celtic, Maley and team mates who had no respect for him, stormed out. By sheer chance, there was no-one like Willie McStay or Willie Maley around to dissuade him, and before anyone knew where he had gone, he was on his way back to Glasgow.

On the Friday Celtic now had no choice. McInally had gone AWOL yet again, and he had to be suspended yet again. McInally himself shouted that he was refusing to play against Motherwell and that he had resigned from the club. The club contented itself by saying that he was suspended and that Frank Doyle, a reserve who was more of a midfielder than an attacker, would play against Motherwell. Rather to the discomfort of McInally, one feels, Frank Doyle scored a great goal against Motherwell and McGrory scored the other in a fine 2–0 win in a game in which Celtic had to dig deep into their reservoir of character and guts. Peter McGonagle, for example, played heroically with his head bandaged to resist the determined and talented Motherwell side.

Without McInally, Celtic then won their next five games, including the Scottish Cup semi final against Queen's Park to set up the first Old Firm cup final since 1904. Celtic were also now marginally top of the league and had a fine chance of landing their fourth 'double' to emulate the mighty feats of 1907, 1908 and 1914. It was hard to resist the conclusion that Celtic were doing very well without Tommy McInally.

Yet, it was not quite as simple as all that. The success was apparent rather than real. The team had won games, yes, but sometimes very luckily. The semi final against Queen's Park at Ibrox, for example, had seen John Thomson at his brilliant best, as the amateurs had, on occasion, threatened to swamp the Celtic defence, and the other wins had been against opposition like Cowdenbeath and Bo'ness. The team were really missing their 'flair player'. Frank Doyle was competent and hard-working, but he was nothing like Tommy McInally.

Tommy, like Achilles in the Iliad who sulked in his

tent because he did not get his own way with Agamemnon and the rest of the Greeks, really did want to be pleaded with and cajoled. He did not do what he threatened to do – to leave the club or give up football altogether. He missed being the centre of attention all that month of March when Celtic were really doing well. He wanted back.

He made it clear that he was training on his own, or sometimes in the company of Tommy Milligan. Barrhead dog walkers or commuters going for the early morning train would see McInally running round the village, then late at night, the noise could be heard of Tommy's feet on the pavement interrupted occasionally by a cheery wave or exchange of greetings with a neighbour.

It is not clear who made the first move. Was it yet again the contrite, repentant McInally who approached Maley with a 'Ignosce, mihi, pater. Peccavi' (Forgive me, father. I have sinned)? Or did Maley himself feel that McInally in the team would add the icing to the cake and bring off the double in style? Perhaps someone like Tommy Milligan, for example, acted as an intermediary. However, it happened, some time after 31 March when Celtic thumped Bo'ness 4–1 and Scotland beat England 5–1 with the team that became known as the Wembley Wizards, Maley decided that McInally could come back.

The decision was released on Thursday 5 April when *The Evening Times* claimed than the lifting of this suspension, 'will be welcomed by Celtic followers and all those who appreciate McInally's qualities as a player'. It was a disastrous decision which gave Rangers the double and had long-term effects on Celtic, from which it took many years to recover. One often wonders whether the fact that it was Holy Week had some effect on the devoutly Catholic Maley. The players were 100 per cent against this move with even Tommy's friends – Peter Wilson, Jimmy McGrory and Adam McLean – finding it hard to justify his actions, and some of the others simply hostile to the idea of his inclusion. But in 1928 what Maley said, went. It was, after all, the age of the dictators.

Celtic's Easter was therefore a bad one. Black Saturday was indeed just that, as the team went down to Motherwell 1–3, then at the start of Easter week, a Lanarkshire double was achieved when Airdrie beat them 3–1. McInally played in both games, was given some praise for a reasonable showing in a losing cause against Motherwell, but against Airdrie, 'he opened well, but found Crapnell a problem which did not lend itself to easy solutions'. The team, confused, disorientated and unhappy, played like a shadow of how they had played before McInally's return, and it was hard not to see a connection. Without McInally, the team had beaten Motherwell in the Cup, with McInally they had virtually lost the league at Motherwell. The conclusion was obvious. The league had been 'blown' and the supporters were now at a serious stage of depression. And there was still the Scottish Cup Final to come on Saturday.

This particular Scottish Cup Final meant a great deal more to Rangers than it did to Celtic. A quarter of a century had passed since Rangers last won the Scottish Cup in 1903. Apart from the unfortunate business of the 1909 Scottish Cup Final, which ended in a riot, they had lost finals in 1904, 1905, 1921 and 1922, a couple of semi finals, notably the famous one in 1925, and the whole business had become a Glasgow music hall joke, and words like 'curse' and 'hex' were freely used. Shell-shocked victims of the Great War had been unconscious for the past ten years and woke up to find out that Rangers still had not won the Scottish Cup! The Kaiser was exiled in Holland and would only come out of exile when his favourite team, Rangers, won the Scottish Cup – so world peace was guaranteed for a while!

But now in the run up to the final, Rangers were beginning to gain in confidence, particularly as Celtic had now seemingly gifted them the league by their woeful performances over the Easter weekend at Motherwell and Airdrie. The ability of the teams was about equal. It all depended on attitude. The McInally question exercised the minds of the Celtic faithful. Adam McLean had been out injured and this may well have affected Celtic's thinking. But Adam had now recovered and it was rumoured that John McMenemy, who had played well in last year's cup final and on any other time he was given the oportunity, might yet be drafted in to take the place of the quixotic McInally.

Maley made the fateful decision and came down in favour of McInally on the grounds that he was the talis-man who might just make the difference. A crowd of 118,115 turned up at Hampden on a cold but dry day of 14 April 1928 with rain threatening, but being kept away by an east wind. Celtic had the wind in the first half, and honours were even, although McInally, 'with odd flashes of inspiration' and 'flickerings of subtlety' came close on at least two occasions. *The Evening Times* insisted that 'he started well' then made the strange but telling comment 'as if he would lead his line', but then barely mentioned him.

Then about ten minutes into the second half came the mighty moment in Rangers' history when Meiklejohn converted the penalty conceded by a handling offence. Now was the time when Celtic had to fight back, when McInally had to inspire them, when the much maligned, overweight genius had to come good. He failed to do so and McPhail, and then Archibald with two, scored as the Celtic end emptied.

Much has been said about Meiklejohn's nerve in taking the penalty. Not without cause, but too little has been said about Celtic's feeble display. Their attacks were 'hesitant and haphazard'. They were dispirited, downhearted and defeated long before the end of this game with the 'Dark Blue' of *The Dundee Courier*, clearly a Celtic supporter under the guise of neutrality, laying the blame firmly where it should have been laid. Sadly, he commented,

> As an attacking force, Celtic were entirely unimpressive. McInally, on whom so much reliance was placed, was a big disappointment. He did many clever things, showing his customary clever manipulation, but much of his passing was careless, and he did not knit the line together.

Celtic fans now had to thole the jeers of their opponents who thundered out 'The Wells O' Wearie' with a few inane words added about 'papists' and 'fenians' from the western terracing, and indeed throughout Scotland there was a great deal of true colours being shown. Falkirk fans, for example, burst into applause when the telegraph boy signalled the score, and a Queen's Park player pointedly put his foot on the ball and looked up at the score on the board, grinned and continued. A cartoon appeared in *The Evening Times* of a Celtic supporter in tears and gloating Rangers and Queen's Park supporters asking whether he now wished he hadn't lost to Queen's in the semi final? Such things did little to discourage what has become known in recent years as the Celtic paranoia.

Much has also been said to imply that Celtic fans accepted this defeat with good grace and that they were really quite glad for Rangers. Indeed, some of the directors said that, and Maley, astonishingly, in his book *The Story Of The Celtic* gave his account of this cup final between those of 1925 and 1931, two of Celtic's most famous cup finals, as if 1928 was on a par! He would also say: 'It is our proud boast that we can accept defeat in the same spirit as that of victory. As well as the fruits of victory, we must also taste the bitterness of defeat.'

But that was so much cant and hypocrisy in the eyes of the Celtic supporter, and indeed, one hopes, in the innermost feelings of Maley himself. The 1928 Scottish Cup Final defeat hurt the supporter. Those of us who lived though the awful days of 1963 and 1990 will empathise. In 1928 the scapegoat was the obvious one. But the Celtic supporter (clearly a school teacher) in *The Evening Times* who wrote the column 'Through Green Glasses' said,

> Our friends have poked fun at us for 'pardoning' Tom McNally (sic). Well, similarly placed, what would they have done? Tommy may have been a difficult lad to deal with, but whatever studies he has collected, he certainly knows his football lessons.

Maybe so, but what about life lessons?

The season now fizzled out slowly and painfully. On the Wednesday after the cup final, only 3,000 turned up at Parkhead to watch Celtic play St. Johnstone in a meaningless game. But McInally was 'in good humour'. The trouble was that no-one else was. He scored two goals, one of them an individual effort through a Perth defence who were clearly afraid of him, but it was clear that the spirit had been knocked out of the Celtic team, so much so that the following day *The Evening Times* made the point: 'subtract McInally from the Parkhead game and there is mighty little left.'

But there was still one chance remaining for McInally. Rangers still had to be faced in the Glasgow Charity Cup semi final at Parkhead on 5 May. The omens were not good – Celtic had struggled to beat Bohemians in a friendly in Ireland, had drawn 3–3 with Partick Thistle (in a game which at least had some good goals) and had guaranteed Raith Rovers' escape from relegation by unaccountably going down 0–3 to them at Parkhead. (Bo'ness, the team relegated instead of Raith Rovers, were distinctly unimpressed by this, but it was probably just a poor performance.) For the Glasgow Charity Cup, McInally probably knew that this was now 'make or break' time for him at Celtic Park.

Ironically, he himself played not too badly, but the team went down 0–2. Maley could now no longer defend McInally or retain him at the club. Yet there were other factors to explain Celtic's fall from grace. In the first place, Rangers did indeed have a good team with men like Sandy Archibald, Alan Morton and Bob McPhail, and 'Clutha' in *The Evening Times* laid the blame elsewhere than on Tommy McInally when he made the unpopular but true statement, 'I'm afraid that McGrory has gone dead off'. William 'Peter' McGonagle, the left back who had played heroically in the Motherwell cup tie with his head bandaged, had been injured in the Motherwell league game and had missed the Airdrie game and the cup final, leaving the inexperienced John Donoghue to take the left back slot. But these were poor excuses and did little to help. The Celtic depression was profound and long lasting.

There was also, according to Maley and the Celtic directors, a financial problem. This was not always easy to swallow, especially when one thought of their share in the huge gate of the Scottish Cup final, but generally gates were not high (13,684 was the home average for Parkhead in season 1927/28 according to David Ross's excellent *The Roar of The Crowd*) and Celtic needed a new stand on the London Road side of the ground, as the Grant Stand was fairly obviously falling apart. Clearly, players would have to be transferred and the wage bill reduced. McInally was the obvious first choice.

McInally was sold to Sunderland in May for a fee normally given as £2,500 – a sum that is a little suspicious because it tends to be the fee quoted for any player of that era. It is a nice round sum and one suspects that it may have its genesis in some newspaper office. Neither club is ever keen to divulge intimate financial details to the press and sometimes the scribes have to be creative. McInally himself would claim not to know the price concerned. In any case it matters little. Celtic had probably decided that McInally would have to go, whatever the price offered.

Although everyone said that McInally would have to go, the actual circumstances took everyone by surprise. Sunderland had just escaped relegation from Division One and were obviously determined that this would never happen again. They had a new manager in Johnny Cochrane, one time of St. Mirren and thoroughly aware of the sheer talent of McInally. Tommy was at Parkhead on Friday 25 May, watching his old school team St. Mungo's playing Whitehill in the Scottish Secondary Shield final when he was invited to talk to the representatives of Sunderland. *The Glasgow Herald* for Saturday 26 May records laconically, 'We are officially informed that Tom McInally the well-known Celtic player was last night transferred to Sunderland'. (With unconscious irony, that same newspaper that same day had an article entitled 'The Insidious Effects of Alcohol'.) The Scottish Junior cup final was played the following day at Hampden when a large crowd saw Maryhill Hibs beat Burnbank Athletic 6–2. The talk of the day however was Tommy McInally.

James Handley in *The Celtic Story* said,

His (McInally's) going provoked the customary ululations from the lads at the wailing wall. It was the departure of the team's best forward. Celtic were now sheep without a shepherd. How could one visualise a successful forward line without its purveyor-in-chief ... But a discontented player, whether he is irked with the management or with his remuneration, is no asset to a club and does no good by remaining on its books.

He was soon followed to Wearside by Adam McLean. Maley also made despicable money-grubbing attempts to sell Jimmy McGrory (on a trip to Lourdes on which McInally was also going until his transfer to Sunderland compelled him to call off) and John Thomson, as profound depression took over his judgement. Neither McGrory nor Thomson wanted to go, however, both of them being committed Celtic players. But if there was any regret about Tommy's departure, it was tempered with realism. Maley had tried so hard for Tommy McInally. More than once, he had gone the extra mile for the boy that he loved. The boy had let him and the Celtic loving part of Scotland down – and very badly.

When the *Celtic Football Guide* appeared in late July 1928, Maley thundered,

> We should have swept the boards but points and games were lost foolishly ... McInally defaulted yet the team picked up and the new spirit was exemplified by McGonagle's playing with a bandaged head in the defeat of Motherwell. Nonetheless we did not deserve to survive against Queen's Park in the semi final and April was a bleak month of staleness. We became a 45-minute team, unable to fight back against Rangers in the final. McInally's transfer wipes out his connection with the club that made him and the nature of the transaction relieved us of any financial obligations towards him. Our attendances have fallen and we have lost the real Celtic following of years ago, equally serene in victory and defeat just as long as they had the green and white to support.

Maley's pain was there visible to all. The 'delighted for Rangers' sort of cant that was put out for public consumption in April and May had now gone.

Naturally he eschewed his own misjudgements, but his frustration was clearly as deep as that of all the support. The bitterness was all the more obvious in that he had clearly brought misfortune upon himself.

There will always be personality clashes in football teams, and indeed in all institutions. But it is up to individuals to bury differences, to realise that the team is more important than the individual concerned. McInally simply did not do that in 1928, causing all sorts of distress to the support. A parallel can perhaps be found in this in Yorkshire cricket of the late 1970s and the early 1980s where Geoff Boycott was the cause of so much discord as, year after year, the feud between Boycott and the rest of the world went on. It was hardly surprising that Yorkshire did not do very well during those years, and the similarities between McInally and Boycott are striking.

McInally was now off to a fresh start. One wonders, in passing, how his mother, who had been so reluctant to see him leave Glasgow in the past, reacted to his going this time. She was probably wise enough to realise that there could be no real future for him with Celtic and that a move from Glasgow was imperative if he were to continue his professional career. In any case, the move did not last long, and Tommy pointedly made it clear that he would make no permanent move to Sunderland. He would live in first-class hotels and in good lodgings, but his home was in Barrhead.

7

International Career

Tommy McInally only played twice for Scotland, both games in the calendar year of 1926 and both, curiously enough, at Ibrox. There were those who thought that he should have played more often and it is undeniably true that, if he had behaved himself, he certainly could have. Oddly, he never played for the Scottish League, often regarded as a step towards a full international cap.

In the 1920s playing for Scotland was looked upon as a great honour. The modern concept of developing an 'injury' to dodge playing for Scotland in order to be fit for a big club game a few days later would have been totally alien to most players of McInally's age. One says 'most' because there is a certain amount of evidence to suggest that Bill Struth of Rangers was not above encouraging men like Meiklejohn and McPhail to exaggerate an injury, thereby missing a trip to Wembley in order to be fit for a Scottish Cup Final the following week. Indeed McPhail admits as much in his book *Legend*. And on one famous occasion Alex James of Arsenal, under pressure from a little emotional blackmail from his manager Herbert Chapman, turned down the chance of playing for Scotland because of 'injury' and played for Arsenal that very day. Hughie Gallacher also occasionally turned down the chance to play for Scotland. But for most players, playing for Scotland meant everything, the game against England particularly so.

It was often said that Celtic players were less committed to playing for Scotland than other players. This is nonsense. It was certainly true that, up to the 1960s, Celtic players in Scotland were on the receiving end of a fair amount of abuse from Rangers fans who made up a disproportionate section of the crowd as Celtic fans (many of them second generation or even first generation Irish) tended to stay away from Scotland games. But the idea that Celtic players were discriminated against, however widely believed by the fans and even by the Celtic establishment, is hardly justified (except in the case of Jimmy McGrory) by the facts.

The choosing of the Scottish team was a particularly haphazard and quixotic business. There was no international manager and selection was in the hands of an august body of men called 'The Selectors', usually seven men who were directors of clubs, although not always the best teams in Scotland. What usually happened was that the selectors would meet about a fortnight before the game, the chairman would say 'goalkeeper', a name or two would be suggested and then, if there was no unanimous agreement, a vote would be taken, before moving on to 'right back'.

The amazing thing was that this system worked and Scotland in the 1920s were more often than not the champions of Britain. In 1921 and 1925, for example, they had beaten all three British countries and thus could lay a reasonable claim to being the champions of the world. What this says about the other three nations, one is not sure, but the selector system certainly seems, eighty years on, to have been an astonishingly amateurish way of running things. Naturally, each selector would back a man from his own club or someone who had impressed him recently and there was no idea of forward planning or policy for the future.

The selectors would normally be men of middle age, respectable members of the community, enthusiastic amateurs whose commitment and patriotism could not be faulted. They would be members of the establishment, possibly even elders of the Church of Scotland – something that the Celtic community would not be slow to latch on to if they wished to cry 'foul' about any team selection.

The system naturally had its critics. Those who wished to see discrimination did so. Supporters of Edinburgh teams thought there was a bias towards Glasgow (they always do!) and small teams felt that their man was cold-shouldered in favour of someone who happened to play for a bigger team. And Celtic fans in particular had a justified point in their complaints about the frequent ignoring of Jimmy McGrory who, at the height of his powers, was never chosen to play at Wembley! In 1930, 1932, 1934 and 1936, he was ignored. Yet this was the man who had scored winning goals for Scotland at Hampden in 1931 and 1933, the latter occasion being credited for the creation of the Hampden Roar! It is hardly surprising that of Scotland's visits to Wembley without McGrory in the early 1930s, three were heavy defeats and the other was a rather lucky draw!

On the other hand, many Celtic players were chosen for Scotland in McInally's time – Willie McStay had been captain and there were also Scottish caps awarded to men like Joe Cassidy, Adam McLean and Peter Wilson. Any complaints, therefore, should perhaps be laid at the door of incompetence and inconsistency rather than at the portal of any sinister Freemason conspiracy.

There was also the 'Anglo' argument. How far should Scotsmen who played for English teams be allowed to play for Scotland? Often, English teams solved this problem for Scotland by saying that they would not allow their players to play for Scotland that day, as they had a game. Sometimes to their shame, even some Anglos themselves turned down the chance of playing against Ireland and Wales, although playing against England would remain the pinnacle of the dreams and aspirations of most players.

The selectors, being the sort of man that they were, would lay great store on things like dress, deportment and behaviour, and this possibly counted against McInally. McInally's wild and erratic behaviour with both Celtic and Third Lanark prevented him from earning any caps before 1926, but in the early months of 1926, his form was superb and he simply could not be ignored. Thus it was that the team for the game against Ireland on 27 February 1926 at Ibrox contained Tommy McInally who would play at inside left alongside his Celtic team mate Adam McLean. This was significant in the selectors' minds for McInally had a tremendous understanding with Adam, and the left wing was commonly referred to as 'the Celtic wing'. Two other Celtic players were included in the team – captain Willie McStay, and Peter Wilson. Peter was also making his international debut that day, and it was also much deserved.

Indeed the Scottish team simply teemed with talent. Hughie Gallacher, once of Airdrieonians but now of Newcastle United, led the forward line, and the right winger was Alex Jackson, once of Aberdeen but now of Huddersfield Town, the team which would that year win the English League. The team was Harper (Arsenal); McStay (Celtic) and Hutton (Aberdeen); Wilson (Celtic); McDougall (Airdrieonians) and Bennie (Airdrieonians); Jackson (Huddersfield Town), Cunningham (Rangers), Gallacher (Newcastle United), McInally (Celtic) and McLean (Celtic).

So how would McInally, a man of indubitable Irish descent and sometimes open IRA sympathies, cope with playing for Scotland, a Protestant country, at Ibrox, the centre of Protestantism against his own people, it was asked? Very well, was the answer. In the first place, the Irishmen he was playing against tended to be the Orange men from the north and, in any case, Tommy was undeniably Scottish with his Glasgow patter and humour. Like most footballers, he hated discrimination and bigotry, however much he was aware of it and even made jokes about it. There would be no more committed Scotsman than Tommy McInally.

Scotland had won all three games last season, had last failed to win an international in 1924 at Wembley, and had lost only three games since the Great War. They were not likely to lose to Ireland and didn't on this occasion. A crowd of 30,000 paid one shilling and sixpence each (about eight pence in modern money) to see this game. The receipts are given as £1,180, but this figure is meaningless, for it is not clear whether it includes the stand, or whether it is after expenses and tax. The game was played in the aftermath of heavy rain, which only eased off at about kick-off and the crowd saw a one-sided game which Scotland won 4–0. Playing in all white, Scotland dominated play from start to finish over a weak Irish side which had suffered a few call-offs and had encountered some resistance from English sides who would not release their men.

Hughie Gallacher scored a hat-trick and Andy Cunningham added the other, but *The Scotsman* was damning with faint praise, with such comments as, 'only up to a point were Scotland good', and the apparent hero of the hour, Gallacher, is criticised for being sloppy and not providing the cohesion required for the forward line. One of his goals was offside as well. But 'McLean and McInally comprised the better forward wing and provided some grand football. McLean was full of resource at outside left, and his crossing was outstanding, and McInally was conspicuously successful at foraging.' So, clearly, the hard-to-please but anonymous journalist of *The Scotsman* thought highly of Tommy on this occasion and one would imagine that the 'Celtic wing' of McInally and McLean was all the happier with the 4–0 result, considering that their direct opponent for Ireland was Bert Manderson of Rangers. And at Ibrox at that!

So why didn't McInally retain his place for the big game against England at Old Trafford? There certainly seems to be no reason in terms of any injury, nor is there any reason to assume that there was any misbehaviour when he was with the Scotland squad. He certainly would have met up with Hughie Gallacher, a character with remarkable similarities to himself in terms of sheer footballing ability, allied to the Scottish penchant for self-destruction in terms of 'hitting the bottle', but no scandal or outrageous behaviour seems to have happened, or at least nothing that came to public attention.

In any case, McInally and Gallacher might well not have got on. As any classroom teacher will tell you, there are seldom two out and out clowns in a class. Usually one has to upstage the other, and there was a certain amount of precedent here in Tommy's relationship with the other Gallacher, Patsy of Celtic. It may be that Hughie and Tommy could not really weld together. It was one thing outclassing a poor Ireland side in Glasgow. England in Manchester would be a totally different prospect and, in any case, an away game would necessarily involve at least a couple of nights in a hotel, where all kinds of nonsense might occur with McInally, Gallacher and one or two others. The selectors perhaps did not want to take the risk.

But another factor entered into the equation when the Scottish League played the English League on 13 March at Celtic Park. The Scottish League selectors ignored McInally and went for the Rangers left wing of Tommy Cairns and Alan Morton. They also committed the blunder of playing Adam McLean, a brilliant left winger on the right wing as some sort of experiment.

This folly earned its just reward as the English League won 2–0, but what made matters worse was that Adam McLean, in his new and unaccustomed position, was injured and out of the Celtic team for a few games. *The Scotsman* commented acidly, 'this game was of more value for the selectors in the negative rather than the positive sense'.

Celtic struggled without McLean, although the League Championship of 1926 was in any case more or less won by then. Adam was brought back for a game on Monday 5 April to see if he was fit enough for the Scottish Cup Final five days later. He clearly wasn't, and was ruled out of both the Scottish Cup Final of 10 April and the England v Scotland game at Old Trafford on 17 April. Tellingly, without McLean beside him, McInally had a poor game in the Scottish Cup Final.

The absence of McLean, one feels, affected decisions on McInally. Perhaps the selectors felt that Tommy could only play alongside his club mate Adam McLean. It was true that they had combined well together and it was also true that Adam, a calm and reliable character, did have an effect on keeping Tommy on the straight and narrow, and therefore Tommy would not be invited to join the party without Adam. One would be interested to know what Willie McStay, captain of both Celtic and Scotland, felt about all this (technically the captain took no part in the selection process, but it is hard to imagine that McStay was not at least consulted unofficially), but, in the event, the Scottish left wing was neither the Celtic one of McInally and McLean, nor the Rangers one of Cairns and Morton, but a bizarre one of Andy Cunningham (normally the inside right of Rangers) and Everton's immensely talented Alec Troup. In spite of all this, Scotland won 1–0.

It is hard to imagine McInally not being disappointed at not getting the chance to play against England, although the edge would have been taken off his objection by Scotland's victory. He did play, however, in the first international game the following season against Wales on 30 October 1926 at Ibrox. By good fortune, coincidence or simply because the selectors got it right, the forward line was the same as that which played against Ireland in February in Tommy's previous international. The team was McClory (Motherwell); McStay (Celtic) and Wiseman (Queen's Park); Gibson (Partick Thistle), Gillespie (Queen's Park), McMullan (Manchester City); Jackson (Huddersfield Town), Cunningham (Rangers), Gallacher (Newcastle United), McInally (Celtic) and McLean (Celtic). Scotland won 3–0 before 40,500 who had paid their 'bob and a tanner' (one shilling and six pence) for the privilege.

Scotland won well but McInally's performance in this game seems to have been a matter of some doubt. Some reports said that he 'sprayed passes thoughtfully', others qualified their admiration for his play. *The Scotsman* reported that 'his intentions were clever, but a fair number of his passes were intercepted' and it is noticeable that while McMullan and Jackson were singled out, McInally was not. Still, Tommy would have had every reason to be happy with Scotland's 3–0 victory, two goals being scored by Alex Jackson and the other by Hughie Gallacher.

The next Scotland game was in the spring in Belfast and Tommy's inside left position went to Jimmy

Howieson of St. Mirren. Howieson was a good player and clearly deserved his chance but nothing in Tommy's play or behaviour at this time justified his omission. Indeed, February 1927 was one of the high spots of McInally's career as he was described as 'mastermind McInally' in a 4–2 demolition of Dundee at Dens Park, for example. Significantly, Adam McLean lost his place as well to Rangers' Alan Morton, and the selectors may well have decided to abandon the 'Celtic wing' altogether. Suggestions, however, that this may have been a deliberate policy to exclude Celtic players from playing in Orange Belfast for fear of causing a riot are fanciful. For one thing, Willie McStay was playing and, indeed, was the Scottish captain and there had never in the past been any great discrimination against Celtic players on that account.

On the other hand, Tommy McInally was no ordinary Celt. He made no attempt to hide his sympathies for the IRA, sang all the Celtic supporters songs like 'God Save Ireland' and 'Erin's Green Valleys' at soirees and parties, and might not have had the tact to keep his mouth shut. In addition there were perhaps more general fears about Tommy's behaviour on an away trip. Be that as it may, on the day that the game was being played (26 February) as Scotland beat Ireland 2–0, Tommy was exacting his own form of revenge on Howieson and St. Mirren by travelling to Paisley and playing brilliantly as Celtic won 6–2, laying on several of Jimmy McGrory's four goals. McGrory too, of course, was making his point to the selectors.

Tommy might have expected a game against England at Hampden in early April, but this time the selectors went for Airdrie's Bob McPhail (a good friend of Tommy from his Barrhead days) to partner Alan Morton, and put Adam McLean on the right wing. This ploy had failed for the Scottish League last season and once again the folly of playing Adam McLean out of position on the right wing was apparent and Tommy did well to miss this game, for the team lost a late goal to Dixie Dean and Scotland had the ignominy of losing their first game at Hampden since the stadium opened in 1903. In any case, Tommy was out with a broken nose and could not have played anyway, but the defeat did allow him to claim that Scotland needed him. 'Ye see whit happens whan I'm no' playin!' he would tell all and sundry.

The following season saw Scotland play a game in Wales in the autumn, a game against Ireland in the spring and then a visit to Wembley (games against foreign opposition would not happen for a year or two yet). He could not be considered for the Wales game because he was suspended, having been sent off for arguing with the referee in a game against Rangers. By the spring, Tommy's form, fitness and attitude had deteriorated to such an extent that he could not realistically be considered for another Scotland cap, and yet once again we can speculate on how good the Wembley Wizards might have been if Tommy, fully fit and fully committed, had been on board. He would have been an asset even to them, although, as they won 5–1, they hardly needed him!

As with Celtic, it is undeniably the case that Tommy could have done more for Scotland. As early as 1922, he might have been considered, had he toed the line, and even in his Third Lanark years, when he was physically at the peak of his powers, a little more self-discipline might have worked wonders in the arcane minds of the Scottish selectors. He was definitely unlucky not to get a game against England in 1926 and 1927, but even in 1927 he was still only twenty-seven years old, and his international potential had not yet been realised. But, of course, the tragedy with Tommy was that it never would be.

8

Sunderland

Sunderland are, in the early years of the twenty-first century, a team of chronic underperformers. They have been so for many years. In this they have something in common with their near neighbours Newcastle and the slightly further away Middlesbrough. Nowhere in the British Isles is football talked about so obsessively, and that would include Glasgow and Liverpool, but success in recent decades for any of the three clubs has been elusive. Sunderland's most recent success was winning the English Cup in 1973 – not exactly yesterday! It often seems that the derbies between Sunderland and Newcastle, for all the intense interest that they engender locally, are looked upon by the rest of the country with sublime indifference, for there is almost a certain guarantee that they will have no relevance to the destination of the Premier League. Relegation, perhaps, as in 2009, but not the top of the table.

It is almost as if the Smoggies (Middlesbrough), the Mackems (Sunderland) and the Geordies (Newcastle) have their own mini-league. It is important to them who finishes up highest of the three, and one sometimes feels that this has worked to the detriment of their long-term welfare. Middlesbrough supporters, for example, sing to the tune of 'My Darling Clementine' the inane,

> Build a bonfire, build a bonfire
> And put the Mackems on the top
> Stick the Geordies in the middle
> And burn the f—in' lot!

Occasionally one detects a bit of humour. The Smoggies (Middlesbrough) are so called because of the smog or the fog that hangs over the Teeside area from industrial pollution. Newcastle or Sunderland supporters can therefore sing 'Fresh air, you only need fresh air!'

It has often been suggested, sometimes frivolously, sometimes seriously, that it might be an idea for the three north-east teams to join a Scottish (or rather a North British) league in which attractive fixtures like Celtic v Newcastle United and Sunderland v Rangers would surely appeal to a large audience. The advantage for the big Scottish teams would of course be more competition (rather than the current tedious situation of the SPL being predictably won by either Tweedle-Dum or Tweedle-Dee) and for the three north-east teams there would be a realistic chance of winning a league championship, something that currently does not seem very likely.

This might put an end to the long-term under-achievement of the area. But underachievement was not always the dismal sine qua non of north-east football. Sunderland have won the League Championship on six occasions but five of them were before the Great War and the other was 1936. Round about the turn of the nineteenth to twentieth century it would have been difficult to argue with the contention that the Roker Park outfit were the best team in England, and they came very close in 1913 to landing a league and cup double. They won the league but lost the final of the English Cup to Aston Villa at Crystal Palace. And until 1958 they maintained the proud record of never having been relegated.

The situation with Sunderland in the 1920s was that they were usually respectably placed in the league but never managed to win it. Nor had they ever won the cup. They were a little upset, however, because they were gradually losing out to Newcastle United, who had won the cup in 1910 and 1924 (the second final ever played at Wembley) and the league in 1927, a triumph spearheaded by the great Hughie Gallacher who had joined Newcastle from Airdrie in December 1925. But rivalry between the two clubs remained keen and gates were high. When Tommy McInally joined Sunderland in summer 1928, he was joining a team whose average attendance was 21,411 – a great deal higher than Celtic's 13,684.

They also had a Scottish manager in Johnny Cochrane. A very small but determined man who knew what he wanted, Cochrane had just taken up office in early May 1928, having replaced the long term and very successful manager Bob Kyle, who had been there since 1905. Charlie Buchan, one of Sunderland's best ever players and known to schoolboys in the 1950s as the proprietor of *Charlie Buchan's Football Monthly*, had been offered the job, but declined. Cochrane came from Paisley and had been the manager of St. Mirren from 1916, where he had had his big moments in the winning of the Victory Cup in 1919 and his greatest triumph – the Scottish Cup of 1926 when his team had upset all the odds by beating Celtic.

He would therefore have known all that there was to know about Tommy McInally. His decision (one of his first) to buy Tommy was taken with his eyes wide open. Perhaps he felt that he could handle Tommy as one Scotsman to another. Perhaps he felt that Tommy needed to get away from Glasgow and the occasionally stifling atmosphere of Celtic Park, but, in any case, he decided to take the gamble. It may be that Cochrane envisaged McInally as the Wearsiders' answer to Hughie Gallacher. They were remarkably similar characters in both playing ability and in temperament.

A feature of the success of both Newcastle and Sunderland had been their large Scottish representation. Sunderland had Ned Doig (sometimes called Teddy Doig) the famous goalkeeper, Jimmy Watson and Charlie Thomson and many others, whereas Newcastle had Peter McWilliam, Sandy Higgins, Bobby Templeton, James Hay and, in recent years, Hughie Gallacher. There was therefore nothing new in Scottish players going to that part of the world and, indeed, culturally, Clydeside and Wearside were not too dissimilar in their heavy industries and large working-class populations. In theory, there would be no reason why McInally could not cope with the lifestyle. But McInally was McInally.

However that may be, *The Sunderland Echo* tells us that Cochrane went to Scotland at the end of May 1928 to sign John Liners *(sic)* meaning John Lynas from

Bo'ness, then proceeded to Glasgow to bring off the great coup of Tommy McInally. *The Sunderland Echo* was jubilant and reported that this was the 'greatest hit of the close season', that McInally would bring 'more stability to the front rank', that he was a 'strong bustler' and that he could 'show generalship in the front line'. The journalist had only seen him twice!

Clearly Cochrane felt that McInally would be a good general, for he appointed him captain very early on in the season. McInally, reputedly, was not very enthusiastic about the idea initially, but was talked round. Cochrane possibly felt that McInally would be a good poacher turned gamekeeper and that if he appointed McInally as captain, Tommy would show responsibility. To be fair, this idea did work for a while, but McInally had little staying power. Indeed, this was a pattern of McInally's two spells with Celtic and his time with Third Lanark as well – he would have a good start, but would not be able to maintain it. He was not always totally committed to Sunderland either, as the following tale would indicate.

Patsy Gallacher (not to be mixed up with Celtic's great Patsy Gallacher and often called Paddy Gallacher to avoid confusion) tells a story from his early Sunderland days which perhaps indicates that Tommy's heart still lay with Celtic.

Tommy, who had been one of my boyhood heroes, would have been an earth-shattering success on the stage because he was a real comedian and a marvellous character. In September 1928, almost a year after my arrival at Roker Park, I remember telling Tommy that Sunderland had asked me to sign a full professional contract with the club and that I intended to comply with their wishes. To my utter amazement, Tommy shouted aloud 'Sign for Sunderland . . . don't be so bloody stupid son . . . haven't I told you that Celtic are dead keen to get you . . . and that's a fact!' That outburst landed Tommy in hot water. His words were overheard by Sunderland chief scout Sammy Blyth, and naturally, when McInally was reported, he was hauled over the proverbial coals by club officials less than happy with the fact that their club captain was desperately trying to persuade me to sign for another team.

This story cannot be literally true, for Tommy never swore. Tommy's tirade contained the word 'bloody' and that is presumably an invention of Gallacher. Nevertheless, the story is somehow credible for Tommy would quickly have realised that Sunderland were a long way away from any honours, and that Celtic, for all their travails, were a better bet for young Gallacher than Sunderland. And indeed, Tommy, no matter what had happened, still loved the Celtic. In spite of this, Paddy Gallacher stayed with Sunderland and won the English League in 1936 and the English Cup in 1937.

Tommy's Sunderland debut was on 25 August 1928 at Turf Moor, Burnley. The team went down to a 1–3 defeat, but Tommy is given credit, for 'it was his first game in England'. The team was: McInroy, Murray and England; Clunas, Allan and Andrews; Lynas, McInally, Halliday, Cresswell and Hargeaves. By his second game, however, Adam McLean had joined him from Celtic at Roker Park and the team beat Blackburn Rovers 3–1. McInally's first goal came on 1 September. It was a very impressive 22-yard free kick (after he himself had been fouled) in a glorious 4–0 win over Derby County at Roker Park in front of a crowd well in excess of 30,000. Clearly, however, there had been some rumblings in the city about the abundance of Scotsmen that Cochrane was bringing, for 'Argus' who writes 'Roker Reflections' in *The Sunderland Echo* was moved to say that 'the cry from the terraces of too many Scotsmen does not break much ice' as long as they were of the quality of David Halliday (from Dundee) and the 'Celtic left wing' of Tommy McInally and Adam McLean

Indeed, the cartoonist Preston B. Durey produced a 'Wearside Scottish' drawing with the 'few English orphans' having to brush up on Robbie Burns to make themselves understood. But life was going on well for both McInally and Sunderland until after one bad game at Blackburn Rovers in mid-September, 'Argus' reflected sadly,

> I think McInally will have to appreciate that in the English game it is necessary for an inside forward to go for the ball. He can place the ball as good as any man playing and he has football brains … but the famous Celt would impress us more if he were more persistent in his efforts to get the ball.

This is sadly the beginning of a pattern, that Tommy was a great player but was slow, lethargic and did not work hard enough. There is of course nothing new here. He scored a beautiful goal in a losing cause in a 3–4 defeat to Birmingham City at Roker Park, unleashing 'a storm of cheering' and now and again there were other reports of spectacular play. Once again, there is nothing new here.

He had a good October. McInally 'put his passes well' in the 4–0 defeat of Huddersfield (a good side under Herbert Chapman in the 1920s and champions as recently as 1926), then at Cardiff (who had won the English Cup in 1927), when Sunderland won 1–0, McInally 'generalled the line and placed his passes to some purpose almost every time', then, at the end of the month, a huge crowd of 50,519 saw Sunderland beat Newcastle 5–2 at Roker Park. The much awaited confrontation between Tommy and Hughie Gallacher had to be put on hold, however, for Hughie was away playing for Scotland that day. Hughie had a good day for he scored a hat-trick for Scotland against Wales but the Magpies paid for their magnanimity and altruism in releasing Hughie. They were outclassed by their local rivals and sunk into the relegation zone as the on-song McInally led the Sunderland line brilliantly. For the Mackems, McKay scored two, Halliday another two and Hargreaves one. McInally had a hand in all five goals. The team was:

Sunderland: McInroy, Murray and England; Clunas,
Parker and Andrews; McLean, McKay,
Halliday, McInally and Hargreaves.

But then after being the man 'who made the openings' in the victory over Bury, a couple of poor games, for both Sunderland and McInally, followed, moving 'Argus' to write in a phrase pregnant with undertones, 'Tom McInally will be showing some of his best football on heavy grounds', the clear implication being that the two defeats to Aston Villa and Leicester City were his fault and that his 'best football' had not yet been forthcoming.

Possibly Tommy did read *The Sunderland Echo* and in an undefeated December, the goals kept coming for Davie Halliday with McInally supplying the ammunition and the team began to move up the table. New Year's Day was particularly sweet with a 5–1 win over Arsenal at Roker Park, and the more optimistic of Sunderland supporters were beginning to talk of 1929 being the year in which Sunderland could become the first team in the twentieth century to win a league and cup double – the honour that had eluded them so narrowly in 1913.

But things began to go wrong for the Wearsiders on 12 January 1929 when they went out of the cup at the first time of asking to West Ham United at Upton Park. This was a bad blow to the thousands of Wearsiders who had treated themselves to a weekend in London. For some unexplained reason, but perhaps because of the ill-health of King George V (he recovered, fortunately), the national anthem was played – something that would sit very ill with McInally, one imagines – and then the normally reliable Sunderland goalkeeper Albert McInroy made an error which cost Sunderland the game. McInally tried hard to rally the troops and twice had shots which went narrowly over the bar, but it was all in vain.

This defeat hit the fragile McInally hard, for he had wanted an English Cup medal to go with his Scottish one of 1927, but for a spell the good form continued in the league and the left flank of McInally and McLean excelled as they beat Portsmouth 5–0 in early February. He picked up a leg injury in the next game as they lost to Birmingham, and then missed a couple of games, but was back in early March for the run in to the league championship.

Sunderland were two points behind Sheffield Wednesday (whom they had beaten 4–3 on a snowy day at Roker on 19 January) as they beat Cardiff City 1–0 on 2 March. At this stage, Tottenham Hotspur put in a bid for Tommy, but the directors turned it down flat. They would very soon have cause to regret this rejection of the chance of making money out of McInally. 'Argus' mused inconclusively in his 'Roker Reflections' about him at this point:

> Tom McInally does not put in 90 minutes strenuous football and though he plays a backward-forward game more often than not, he does not possess tackling power. On the other hand, with one kick, McInally can produce more favourable position than 20 yards dribble.

Sunderland's key day in this season was the derby game at St. James Park. In glorious spring weather on 9 March with over 55,000 inside the ground and hundreds more perched precariously on roofs at the Leazes End of the ground, Sunderland had the chance to top the table. Unfortunately, they equalised three times but still went down 3–4 at the end. The goal was bizarre and involved McInally. It was a throw-in near the Sunderland goal. Tommy took it, and it was a foul throw. While Tommy stood arguing and the Sunderland defence hesitated, a Newcastle player took the throw and sent the ball to Hughie Gallacher who scored the winner.

'Argus' took Tommy to task. He wrote that anyone can make a mistake with a foul throw, but why was

McInally taking it? It was not his job. In any case, McInally was not fast enough, nor was there any tackling ability. 'Argus' then went on to attack McInally indirectly by praising his friend Adam McLean. Adam, wrote 'Argus', 'possibly thinks of his old love, the Celtic, but to McLean, Sunderland is more than a name and a place where he draws the necessaries for food and shelter'. It did not take a genius to work out what he was really saying here.

Tommy was injured for the game on 16 March, one presumes, and then on 23 March there was no game for it was cup semi final day in both Scotland and England. It was no secret that Tommy went back to Glasgow to see Celtic play Kilmarnock at Ibrox. It would be a painful occasion for him for Celtic lost 0–1 to the excellent Kilmarnock side who would beat Rangers in the final, but Tommy made sure he was noticed in the stand at Ibrox as he held court about Sunderland, Johnny Cochrane and how they might yet win the English league, while also being big enough to admire the work of his successor at inside left, Peter Scarff.

There then followed two games which pushed him beyond the point of no return with Sunderland fans. There was a 1–2 home defeat to Leicester City which was bad enough, but then there was also a poor game in a friendly against St. Mirren (which Johnny Cochrane had arranged when he changed clubs). McInally played in both games, looked lethargic and listless and was roundly booed by the fans on both occasions. The Sunderland fans, like those of Celtic, were very hard on someone who, they knew, could play better – but that did not excuse the ludicrous charges of 'not trying' against St. Mirren because they were Scottish!

'Argus' was moved to deliver a round of the guns at both the fans and at McInally:

> It seems to me that the Sunderland crowd has taken up a very hard and unsportsmanlike attitude to one player – I refer to Tom McInally. I hold no brief for the ex-Celtic player who in my opinion has great football brain power, but has not shown that he can stand 90 minutes of strenuous English League football. But no player can possibly have his heart in the game if his efforts are received with derision by a section of the crowd.

Clearly McInally's fall from grace had been sudden, dramatic and profound. From the heady days of around the New Year when songs about him had been sung – the old Celtic ones with a few changes –

> He'll open up the door and he'll start the Roker Roar
> Tommy , Tommy, Tommy McInally

He was now the target of the boo boys. He had not helped himself by his behaviour – he had had a few wild nights, it was said (some, it was rumoured with horror, in Newcastle with Hughie Gallacher!), and by his frequent sojourns back to Glasgow – something which tended to suggest that his heart was not with Sunderland. He had made no attempt to find a house in Sunderland and lived in a first-class hotel where, as he himself said, 'the steaks and eggs were awfu'guid'. Now that things were beginning to go wrong for Sunderland in their league title chase, a scapegoat was required. As at Celtic, Tommy fitted the bill.

167

Two games remained to be played by McInally that season, one good and one bad. Revenge was gained on West Ham United for the cup exit in a 4–1 win at Roker Park in which McInally was 'only moderate in the first half, but a lot better in the second', but then in a 0–5 cave-in away from home to Sheffield United, Tommy had the indignity of not having his name mentioned at all in *The Sunderland Echo*.

Yet, overall, it had not been a bad season at Roker. Some good football had been seen, Sunderland had finished fourth in the league – a huge improvement on 1927/28 when they had flirted with relegation – and the gates had averaged 24,863. Finances were sufficiently good for the Sunderland directors to approach the famous ground designer Archibald Leitch to design and erect a new stand in the image of those at Ibrox and Goodison over the close season. As McInally found with Celtic, though, a new stand was often in the 1920s paid for by the shedding of players!

But the close season saw McInally take drastic measures in a belated attempt to resurrect his career. He began a crash diet – always a dangerous option – and on 18 June, *The Glasgow Observer* reported that he was in a Glasgow nursing home after the dramatic loss of a stone and a half. Whether this was the whole truth or not, or whether there was an alcoholic component to this illness, we do not know, but no more is heard of this business and by the beginning of September he was back at Roker to begin the new season.

He would play in only four games that season. On the day that the new stand was declared open, McInally (no longer captain, for Jock McDougall, another member of the Airdrie diaspora, had that office now) played well in a good 5–2 win over Manchester City. Tommy was able to offer his jesting criticism of the new stand: 'I dinnae like it. It's ower like Ibrox!' But after three defeats he disappeared under a welter of criticism. Against Arsenal on 21 September he put in some hard work but, there was an absence of accuracy in placing the ball, and when that is not there, then McInally's utility as part of the combination is seriously reduced and the following week, in his last game for the club (a 1–2 defeat by Aston Villa), he was described as having no staying power.

He then disappeared, but so did several other players too. The Wall Street Crash had not yet hit the North East (it would very soon) but there was already a fair amount of unemployment in the area and Sunderland had the extra burden of the new stand to pay for. This meant that players had to be sold. Davie Halliday went, so did Albert McInroy (to Newcastle United!) and the directors would have loved to be able to sell McInally. As early as the previous May, it now emerged, they had let it be known that he might be for sale, but no-one was interested.

Eventually a decision was made to cut their losses that they were sustaining on McInally's wages and to offer him a free transfer. McInally had in fact raised the issue first by complaining to the directors that he was not being given a game and he caused a little gratuitous offence by using the word 'novices' to refer to the young men that were replacing him. So a free transfer was offered, at first declined, but then accepted on 11 November 1929.

Depending on the spin that one puts on this, one can see it positively that McInally was 'relieved of his responsibilities', 'allowed to negotiate his own terms with some other club', or quite simply 'sacked'. *The Sunderland Echo* commented that this was probably the first time that this had happened in the history of Sunderland with a player of such a reputation. McInally had been a Scottish internationalist little more than three years previously. He was given some credit for the team's revival in the earlier part of season 1928/29, but only 'occasional glimpses of the real artist' had been seen, for he could not sustain effort for ninety minutes. It was speculated that 'McNally' *(sic)* would return to Scotland where the pace was slower – a questionable assumption, it would have to be said.

'Argus' had one final dig at him in 'Roker Reflections'. He had heard a story that McInally arrived back in Glasgow, 'rather like Santa Claus laden with presents from his admirers south of the Tweed'. This caused amusement, 'Argus' reported, in the Sunderland dressing room, for a free transfer was 'hardly a present worth boasting'. At this point, McInally disappeared from Sunderland, apparently for ever. Although his death in 1955 was mentioned in *The Sunderland Echo*, there was no obituary. The many excellent histories of Sunderland F.C. either mention him only in passing or do not mention him at all. He was not a great figure in Sunderland's history. The shame is that he should have been and, indeed, he could have been.

Sunderland would move on to have a revival in the 1930s with players like Paddy Gallacher, Bobby Gurney, Sandy McNab and Raich Carter, and win the league in 1936 and the cup in 1937, thus guaranteeing Johnny Cochrane immortality on Wearside. Cochrane would need time to build that team up following the compulsory stripping of assets in 1929, but he did so. McInally, a man little given to jealousy or bitterness, would have been glad to see that. He remained on good terms with Cochrane, as indeed he did with Willie Maley. He would have loved 1937 when both his teams won their respective cups, but would have been even happier one feels on 6 October of that year when Celtic beat Sunderland 2–0 at Roker in what was called 'the cup winners' match'.

McInally's serious footballing days after he left Sunderland are barely worth mentioning. He had a few insignificant months with cash-strapped Bournemouth and the even more impecunious Morton. Then, in 1931, he crossed the Irish Sea to play for Derry City. He made much play of how he would be accepted in that Orange stronghold – in fact even in 1931 Derry City were supported by the Catholic community rather than the Protestant one – but he did play in an Irish Cup semi final where they were beaten by a Ballymena side which contained his old friend Joe Cassidy and ex-Ranger Billy McCandless. He did not stay around long after that and was soon back in Scotland in his beloved Barrhead.

McInally had a big day back at Celtic Park on 4 January 1932. It was Patsy Gallacher's benefit, a game between a Celtic/Falkirk Select (Celtic and Falkirk were the two teams that Patsy had played for) against the Rest of the Scottish League. Tommy appeared to act as linesman. Dressed in plus fours, and now built like the gable end of a house, Tommy played his part in the light-hearted occasion, catching the ball when it went out of play, stuffing it down his jacket and waddling like a pregnant woman. The crowd did not always enjoy this nonsense, but for Tommy it was great fun and also a chance to show that although Patsy Gallacher had once been his rival for the attention of the crowd, there was no grudge. In fact, he would on several occasions play for Patsy's Charity XI in light-hearted games against 'The Police' or some other Charity XI.

Then on 21 January 1933 at Volunteer Park, Armadale, the local team in their veritable death throes, sprang a surprise. The 'Dale were bankrupt and had been removed from the Scottish League because of their inability to pay the 'guarantee' (the minimum amount to cover the away team's expenses) but they were still in the Scottish Cup. Their opponents were Dundee United, and the reporter of *The Sporting Post* had a real scoop on his hands for he sent back to Dundee the headline: 'Tommy McInally Turns Out For Armadale'. Five hundred people were there at the start of the game, but rumours had spread round the village and the crowd doubled to 1,000 before full time. Sadly, Armadale lost 0–2 but Tommy, presumably playing as an amateur (for Armadale had no money!) had one shot which flashed past the post. Both Armadale and Tommy McInally said goodbye to senior football that day, although Tommy would now and again turn out for Nithsdale Wanderers between 1933 and 1937, sadly after the Sanquhar side had lost their Scottish league status.

9

Assessment

Tommy McInally died (of course the death certificate called him Bernard) at 3.15am on Thursday 29 December 1955 at 111 Paisley Road, Barrhead only a few days after his fifty-sixth birthday. He had been suffering from 'carcinoma of the fauces', commonly known as throat cancer, for two years. He was described as a commercial traveller and as single, his death being signed by his brother Arthur who was present at the time.

The event happened too late for the morning newspapers of 29 December, although it appeared in a few of the evening ones, and in all the morning papers of 30 December. A few of them got facts wrong, such as reporting that Tommy died 'in a Glasgow hospital'. *The Glasgow Herald*, however, carried a death notice which said:

McINALLY – At Crinan, Paisley Road, Barrhead on 29th December 1955, Tommy McInally ex-Celtic FC RIP. Requiem Mass tomorrow (Saturday) at 9.30am in the Parochial Church, Water Road, Barrhead, funeral thereafter to St. Conval's Cemetery, Barrhead.

173

The Mass was held early on the Saturday to allow members of the Celtic party to attend and then to proceed to Dumfries, where they were playing Queen of the South that afternoon. His brothers John (commonly called Jake) and Arthur were the chief mourners.

Because Scotland was girding itself up for its New Year celebrations (a huge event now, but even bigger in the 1950s when Christmas had not yet emerged as a rival attraction), Tommy's death possibly did not get the attention that it might otherwise have had, but tributes were paid to him. Jimmy Brownlie, who had been the goalkeeper of Third Lanark in the 1920s at the same time as Tommy, said, for example in *The Dundee Courier*,

> There is no doubt that he was one of the great personalities of Scottish football. He was a pawky lad and a favourite wherever he went. His ball control was a treat.

The football correspondent of *The Glasgow Herald* (Cyril Horne) said that,

> Tommy McInally was one of football's characters – a tremendous personality on and off the field. That he was a great player there is no doubt; that he could have been even greater, there is equally little doubt. He believed that there was a place for fun in the game, and his idiosyncrasies did not always suit club policy. Accordingly, he did not gain as many material rewards from the game as he might have done. No player however derived more enjoyment from his football, and in the days when his playing career was over, he did not hesitate to say that he 'lived' in football.

Bob McPhail, the Rangers legend who was a great friend of Tommy and also came from Barrhead, said,

In his early days, Tommy was tall and slim and a prolific scorer. In his later days, he was overweight but a masterly inside forward with deft, creative touches which made him one of the best play-makers in the game. Indeed his extra weight proved an advantage, for he was quite brilliant at shielding the ball as he balanced himself to make a telling pass.

Bob, of course, played against Tommy in his career for Airdrie and Rangers.

The Glasgow Herald related an amusing interlude in its editorial room the day of Tommy's death. One of the editorial team, clearly a venerable Celtic supporter, was asked to name the best Celtic team that he had seen. He blustered and asked, 'Good gracious, man, are you totally beyond the reach of education? Can you not assimilate even the bare essentials of history?' before 'with the lilt of an Ossianic saga' lapsing into 'Shaw, McNair and Dodds; Gilchrist, Cringan and McMaster; McAtee, Gallacher, McInally, Cassidy and McLean'. The learned sage then entertained them all with stories of Tommy sitting on the ball, telling the referee that there was a better show on at the Empire when sent to the pavilion and so on. Disingenuously, one of the junior reporters then asked whether he had not played for Partick Thistle?

In truth, not a great deal is known about Tommy after his career fizzled out in the early 1930s but he seems to have earned his living on a haphazard casual basis as a commercial traveller, a scout for Celtic (from 1948 onwards), a freelance writer for newspapers (probably not as a 'ghost' because, as his memoirs show, he had a good literary style and would have enjoyed delivering personally his own trenchant opinions), and as a comedian, singer and entertainer in various Glasgow nightclubs. Jimmy Sirrel, for example, talks of seeing him in the Naval Club in Elmbank Crescent where Tommy greeted him with 'Young Sirrel, young Sirrel do you want to buy me a drink?', and at one point he also owned a small club near La Scala in Paisley. But this is hardly a complete picture. What, for example, did he do in the Second World War? He would have been 40 in the first winter of the war, so he was probably too old to serve in the forces (in the same way as he had been too young to serve in the Great War) but he would have had to have done something for the war effort. The name 'Tommy McInally' would not have been big enough to get him out of that!

It is possible that he went to Ireland where he would almost certainly have had some distant relations. Ireland was neutral, and quite a few of those who were disinclined to serve the British Empire were able to disappear 'for the duration' to the land of their forefathers. But we have no evidence. Tommy's whereabouts during the years 1939 until 1945 remain, like so many years of Tommy's later life, a mystery.

His commercial travelling was in whisky, mainly. A commercial traveller was someone who went round the country working for various firms and visiting shops to see how much of any given commodity they were likely to need. Nowadays, this is all done by e-mail, fax or telephone, but in the 1950s, a good commercial traveller was worth his weight in gold. Tommy could drive, and did at one point own a Citroën (the only person in Barrhead to do so and Bob McPhail told the story of how someone put a dead bird in the engine, then asked to see the engine – just to see the look on Tommy's face), but most of his travelling would have been done by train. Tommy, naturally sociable and very keen for everyone to know who he was and to talk about football, was well suited for this job. There would be no end of people who would want to talk to him and to buy him a drink in return for some cheery conversation from the legendary Tommy McInally. It was often said of Tommy that 'he never bought a drink in his life', on the grounds that there were always loads of people prepared to do that for him.

His travels round the country would have had two important side effects for Tommy. One was that he would always be on the lookout for young football players. He was also working as a scout for Celtic and getting tip offs for young stars about whom he could inform his old colleague and friend Jimmy McGrory who was then the manager of Celtic. It was Tommy, for example, who first drew the attention of Celtic to Alec Byrne, a good player for Celtic in the late 1950s and early 1960s. The other was that he learned a great deal of local stories and songs which he could use in his other capacity as singer and entertainer. A man from Forfar, for example, was once astounded to hear the great Tommy McInally sing a local Forfar song called 'Here's to Bummie on the Hill', a somewhat bawdy song with a deliberate double entendre of 'Bummie' which has its obvious significance, but is also the shortened name for the local hill called Balmashanner.

His fourth source of income was writing for newspapers on football. This was a phenomenon which still occurs today, in which a famous name of the past writes a column. Sometimes it is made up in the office and possibly the famous columnist does not even see the piece before it appears as his column in return, of course, for a fee. Not so in Tommy's case. Tommy enjoyed writing about the game. His articles for the *Scottish Football Digest* were always entertaining and full of insights into his character. Being Tommy McInally, of course, meant that he could never resist playing up to the gallery in his writing in the same way as he did in his playing!

In the lead-up to the 1954 World Cup, Tommy, already a sick man, thundered a warning to Scotland about how good the Uruguayans would be. Tommy was one of the very few players around who had the slightest experience of South American football, for he was drawing on his experience of thirty years previously, when he had been in Argentina with Third Lanark. The South Americans had been far better than the arrogant Scots had assumed they would be. Sadly, Tommy's siren warning availed naught. Scotland were defeated 0–7 by Uruguay, their cause not helped by the resignation of manager Andy Beattie before the game!

He remained volubly opposed to any idea of 'coaching', except for youngsters. Having been a brilliant player himself, he resented the idea that professionals needed coaching and stated rotundly in one of his many articles for the *Scottish Football Digest*,

> Football games should be played on the field, not in flights of imagination. I believe in coaching, but I believe in true coaching, as far as the adult is concerned can only be had on the field of play by playing alongside the better and more experienced player.

Like many of the McInally family, Tommy would never use bad language. It is probably true to say that he had many of the other vices of drinking, over-eating, smoking, womanising, gambling and sloth – but swearing he would neither indulge in, nor tolerate in others. 'You'll go to the big bad fire,' he would frequently say if he heard any foul language. It is indeed odd, but it also does him credit, that he managed to retain this virtue, considering that he spent his life in so many environments like football clubs, pubs and nightclubs, where foul language is so prevalent and even second nature to so many people. In particular, it is hard for us to imagine how he could have been such a successful entertainer and joke teller without using the occasional bad word.

But I think some of this can be explained by the basic good nature and essential virtuous qualities of Tommy McInally. Tommy was not a bad person. He was passionate, quick-tempered on occasion, lacking in respect to authority and profoundly weak and easily led to mischief, but he would seldom go deliberately out of his way to upset anyone. He realised that bad language could upset someone, and also realised that swearing was not anything that one had to do. It did not make you more of a man if you could use bad words.

He did, however, occasionally let his tongue get the better of him. One verbal indiscretion led to a spectacular family feud. *The Barrhead News* of 21 February 1930 tells the story of a family spat which got out of hand and ended up in court. It concerned Tommy's cousin who became a well known and much loved Barrhead character. He was headmaster at the local primary school, St. John's, for over thirty years and who would later become

179

Provost of Barrhead. He had become a teacher through the university route, something that was not necessarily all that common in the 1920s and 1930s. Tommy had one day, ill-advisedly (and possibly when under the influence of strong drink) said that someone had impersonated this fellow when exam time came round, and had sat the exams for him. This was a bizarre accusation – presumably a joke – and one would have liked to have known if Tommy had any evidence for this. His cousin duly sued Tommy for slander, demanding £200. The case was settled out of court – one suspects that the rich uncles might have played a part here – but relationships between Tommy McInally and his cousin, possibly Barrhead's two best known personalities, were never quite the same again, one would have imagined.

No evidence exists of there ever having been any long-term romantic relationship with a woman. He was certainly never married, and he was simply of the wrong age, the wrong religion and the wrong personality to have co-habited with a woman. He had strong sexual urges, no doubt, but lacked the ability to commit himself to any long-term relationship. He simply was not responsible enough. Women did feature in his life, of that we can be sure, and it is at least possible that one or two of his mysterious disappearances were caused by a lady, but there was nothing long term. Perhaps his footballing life would have been different if there had been.

Bob McPhail of Rangers (an excellent source in spite of being on the other side) talked highly of Tommy both as a player and as a man. McPhail's book *Legend – Sixty Years at Ibrox* is a decent book written by a decent man. It is easy to dismiss it as bland, but it is emphatically not that. The high regard in which he held Tommy was entirely genuine, and it is interesting to compare McPhail's feelings of Hughie Gallacher, a team mate of his with Airdrie and Scotland and, at first glance, a man with many similarities to Tommy McInally. McPhail, however, pulled no punches about Hughie Gallacher:

> I didn't like him. He was a selfish wee fellow. He thought of no one but himself. . . . All that mattered to Hughie was Hughie . . . He had a vicious tongue and he used it on opponents. I learned swear words from Hughie I had never heard before. He was a winner on the field, and if he had to upset his opponents to win, then he wouldn't hesitate to do so.

This is in total contrast to the gentle Tommy. He was as good a player as Hughie Gallacher, his lifestyle was equally dissolute and ultimately as unhappy, but Tommy was never vicious or nasty. He was foolish many times, had no real sense of responsibility, was impetuous, couldn't cope with adulation, couldn't cope with discipline – but there was always a sense of humour and a lack of any real unpleasantness. And, of great importance to the church-going McPhail, Tommy did not use bad words!

He was a tremendous prankster. Jimmy McGrory tells the story of how when they were at Seamill Hydro one night before a game, Tommy had smuggled in a bottle of whisky. Many of the guests at the Hydro were old people to whom Tommy was, as always, very courteous, polite and sociable. He noticed that they would fill their cups with drinking water from a tank before retiring for the night, as the rooms did not yet have sinks. Tommy decided that the old folks needed a treat and poured some of his illegal whisky into the tank, then watched as they took their water, drank it, then became noisier, cheerier and even in some cases a little argumentative and pugnacious! McGrory was delighted that Tommy in 1928 cancelled his trip to Lourdes. Jimmy feared that he might do the same with the terminally ill patients in the spa!

Tommy was generous. He had no medals left by the time that he died, for he kept giving them away to friends and even acquaintances, and whenever he met any of his younger relatives, they would be taken to Moni's Ice Cream Shop in Barrhead (Moni was a friend of his) and treated to an ice cream. He also did a great deal of work for charity, in particular for St. Mary's Convent, and would always make sure that some of the Celtic football players put in an appearance at their annual fete. In June 1925, for example, after his return to Celtic but before he had played a game for them, Tommy brought a five-a-side Celtic team to beat the local five 4–1. The five consisted of two reserves, himself, Jimmy McStay and Adam McLean. He also, on another occasion, organised a charity game between Patsy Gallacher's XI and the Barrhead Merchants.

Tommy was not the sort of man who would bear a grudge. If there had ever been any dispute between himself and Patsy Gallacher – and there is no evidence to suggest that there ever had been anything other than healthy professional rivalry – it was certainly quickly forgotten, because, as we have seen, by 4 January 1932, when Patsy was given his benefit by Celtic in the shape of a Celtic/Falkirk XI playing the Scottish League, who appeared as linesman but Tommy McInally? True to character, Tommy stole the show. By then grossly over-weight, Tommy himself made wisecracks to the crowd about Billy Bunter, pregnancy and the half-time pies as he waddled up and down the touchline.

He certainly retained the mutual love and respect of Willie Maley throughout his life, in spite of all that had happened. Writing in the *Scottish Football Digest* of February 1950, McInally said,

> Quite a number of club managers these days are referred to as 'The Boss'. That title was the original possession in foot-ball of Mr. Maley who throughout my wayward career has been a steady friend to me. There is no tribute high enough I could pay him. Looking back there must have been times when I nearly broke his heart. He was often, goodness knows, angry with me, but he always forgave me, his invari-able remark at the forgiveness ceremony being 'You're an awful fellow, Tommy' followed by the comment that he hoped I'd grow up soon. That, no doubt, was in reference to the description applied to me 'Football's Peter Pan'.

It would have to be said that he enjoyed being the centre of attention. People would approach him on the street and say, 'Excuse me, sir, I hope you don't mind me asking but are you Tommy McInally?' He would then say, 'I thocht ye wid never ask . . .' Christmas panto-mimes would always have a reference to Tommy McInally, who was a great friend of Tommy Morgan of 'Clairty, Clairty' fame. When Tommy Morgan, in his role as the pantomime dame, ever had to say the line, 'Who do you think you are?', Morgan would always follow it with 'Tommy McInally?'. And if ever there was a line involving fatness, Tommy would get a mention. For example in *Goldilocks and the Three Bears*, when the bears asked 'Who's been eating my porridge?', the audience would be encouraged to shout out: 'Tommy McInally!'

Jokes about Tommy's gluttony were of course nothing new. The story went that, back in his St. Anthony's days, the officials of the junior club had laid on hospitality in the shape of sandwiches and pies for their players and the opposition for after the game. Tommy sustained an injury with about ten minutes to go and, with the Ants winning comfortably, limped off the field and didn't return. When the rest of the players came off, there was no McInally and no food! Tommy had scoffed the lot! This story is of course unlikely for several reasons – and looks like a story made up years after Tommy had begun to put on weight. In 1918 and 1919 Tommy was a very slim young man and, in any case, given the circumstances of the Great War, there would not have been very much food around!

But Tommy would have done nothing to discourage these stories. There was another that he told himself about the time at Cathkin, in front of a poor crowd, he rose to head a ball, and a well known Cathkin character in the crowd who attended every week no matter how badly the team was playing shouted to Tommy: 'Keep your mouth shut, Tommy, or else you'll think the baw's a dumplin and eat it.' Tommy then replied, 'Naw, it's mair like a Christmas pudding!' Again, a somewhat unlikely tale – but part of the mythology of Tommy McInally.

What cannot be denied is that Tommy did on

occasion at least (if not all his life) drink too much. His putting on of weight in 1927 for example (so pronounced that it is hard to believe that a photograph of Tommy in 1927 is of the same person as a photograph of Tommy in 1919) was almost certainly down to the consumption of beer, added to a reluctance to counteract its effects by training. In later years, he took whisky, it was said, but he would basically drink anything – preferably if someone else was paying!

Tommy retained some of his religious faith. He attended mass and went to Lourdes on at least one occasion. He was all too aware of the weaknesses in his own character, and for that reason he was not inclined to be condemnatory or judgemental of others. Nor would he have had much truck with any sectarian approach to religion. He was far too friendly with men like Bob McPhail of Rangers for that. It would have been difficult to imagine his politics being anything other than Labour (he was also a friend of the great Jimmy Maxton), although in the 1920s, at least, there would have been more than a slight sympathy for Sinn Féin and the IRA as well. He lived long enough to see by 1955 the beginnings of a better life for working people in Glasgow as the Welfare State began to make a difference, but the National Health Service could not do very much to save Tommy.

His sympathies for the IRA would be of the 'armchair soldier' type. Like most Celtic supporters, he would sing songs like 'God Save Ireland', 'The Wearing of the Green', 'Slievenamon' or the rebel song that dominated the singing at Parkhead in the late 1920s and the 1930s, 'Kevin Barry':

In Mountjoy Jail, one Monday morning
High upon the gallows tree
Kevin Barry gave his young life
In the cause of liberty!
Just a lad of eighteen summers
But there's no-one can deny
As he walked to death that morning
Proudly held his head on high!

And he would not be backward in expressing his opinions, but he would have been genuinely horrified by any kind of violence, whether by the Irish rebels or the Black and Tans. He was far too gentle a man for that.

Tommy's memoirs are tantalisingly incomplete. Written in a school jotter in his own handwriting and containing little more than about twenty pages, they are only the start of his autobiography, the foreword of which would have been written by Jimmy Maxton. It is a shame that they were not completed, for there is every indication that Tommy's writing would have been as quixotic and charming as his football playing. Written in the 1930s – certainly before World War Two, for he talks about 'the war' as if there had only been one – his memoirs reveal a certain amount about the man himself. On occasion, they give Tommy's perspective on things. He is, for example, vitriolic about the way that football clubs treat their players, using words like 'abominable' to describe the transfer market and comparing the treatment of players with slaves in ancient Rome. He thinks that footballers should be paid more, and is also of the opinion that footballers should have something other than football, for one never knows when a football player's career is going to end. A football player should make the most of what he has.

Tommy suffered from throat cancer for two years before his death in December 1955. His last two years must have been horrendous. Living in the family home 'Crinan' at 111 Paisley Road, Barrhead and nursed by his sister Sara (sometimes called Hattie) and his brother John (Jake), Tommy paid a large price for his heavy smoking over many years. His brother Arthur told the story of how Tommy begged Arthur to see if he could get stronger pain killers, and his grand-nephew, Tom Higgins, recalls how, as a young boy, he visited Tommy and how Tommy talked, sociable as ever, but had extreme difficulty and pain in so doing.

Tommy would certainly have followed the progress of his beloved Celtic. He was at the Golden Jubilee dinner in 1938 where he famously asked Maley, in his inimitable, impish style, 'Hey, boss, am I getting a bonus for being here?' And he would have been delighted with the team's victory in the Empire Exhibition Trophy a few days earlier. But the team lost more than it won in the late 1940s and early 1950s, although the Coronation Cup in 1953 brought delight to the fans and was followed a year later by a Scottish League and Scottish Cup double. But 1955, the year of McInally's death, saw a horror story of a Scottish Cup Final when the team were a goal up in the last minute against Clyde, then lost a late goal from a corner kick, then lost the replay in the rain the following Wednesday night. The by-now desperately ill Tommy McInally would have been distressed at that. He would probably have been too ill to appreciate the events of Boxing Day 1955 (three days before his death) when Celtic beat Rangers 5–3 in the replay of the final of the Glasgow Cup, the trophy in which McInally himself had starred so prolifically thirty years previously.

Assessments of McInally vary. Even after his death, there was an almost mystical belief in the power of Tommy McInally, as seen in the story of the man whose house was on fire pleading with the firemen to 'save Tommy McInally' – a picture of Tommy which hung over the fireplace which was in danger of being burned or getting wet from the water from the firemen's hoses. Tommy's grand-nephew Tom McInally in his career as a policeman tells the story of the Glasgow drunks, arrested for having had one or two too many on a Saturday night, and bursting out into song at the police station when they discovered that the officer who had arrested them bore the illustrious name of Tom McInally.

Other supporters, while (most of them) aware of Tommy's flaws, nevertheless aver his footballing skill was immense and would compare him favourably with any other footballer that any given World Cup would throw up on television. A piece of skill from the likes of Pele, Cruyff or van Basten would invite comparisons with Tommy McInally and, if there were two veteran Celts, an argument might develop about the relative merits of Patsy Gallacher and Tommy McInally, while a slightly younger Celt might put in a word or two for Charlie Tully or even Jimmy Johnstone.

Tommy's statistics are open to question. It is impossible to say with any degree of certainty how many goals he scored, for example. This is because those who compile statistics of games played in the 1920s are dependent on newspaper reports and sometimes newspaper reports disagree. But using Paul Lunney's *Celtic – A Complete Record 1888–1992*, McInally's Celtic record seems to be as follows:

		Games	Goals
1919/20	Scottish League	32	30
	Scottish Cup	2	2
	Glasgow Cup	3	4
	Glasgow Charity Cup	2	0
	Total	39	36
1920/21	Scottish League	37	28
	Scottish Cup	3	2
	Glasgow Cup	3	2
	Glasgow Charity Cup	2	4
	Total	45	36
1921/22	Scottish League	24	16
	Scottish Cup	3	1
	Glasgow Cup	3	1
	Glasgow Charity Cup	0	0
	Total	30	18
1925/26	Scottish League	37	17
	Scottish Cup	6	5
	Glasgow Cup	3	0
	Glasgow Charity Cup	3	2
	Total	49	24

1926/27	Scottish League	31	8
	Scottish Cup	7	1
	Glasgow Cup	2	1
	Glasgow Charity Cup	1	0
	Total	41	10
1927/28	Scottish League	27	15
	Scottish Cup	4	4
	Glasgow Cup	2	0
	Glasgow Charity Cup	1	0
	Total	34	19
	Grand Total	238	143

James Handley in *The Celtic Story* summed him up,

> ... McInally was a natural footballer and gifted with a streak of real genius. Unorthodox in methods, he puzzled opponents by the unexpectedness of his manoeuvres, and a wide range of football vision enabled him to see two or three moves ahead. He controlled the play with consummate ease and he had a devastating shot with either foot. Moreover he was a personality, a centre of public interest and press rumours and, like Patsy Gallacher, always good for a line in the evening placards.

A neutral source, Hugh Taylor, a journalist with *The Daily Record* and other papers and the editor of *Scottish Football Book* which appeared annually in the 1950s and 1960s, wrote of McInally in his book *Great Masters of Scottish Football*,

> To him flair was all: the shrug of the shoulders, the flick of the hip, the dummy, the careful precision pass, the body

swerve; usually an inside forward, although not always so, he was an expert in altruism. His job was to make goals, not to score them, to hold the ball for the fraction of a second needed for his younger and more virile colleagues to take up position, then slide the ball to the man most likely to be able to shoot without distraction.

Taylor is here clearly referring to the years when Tommy was an inside forward, and not the early part of his career when he was the free scoring centre forward that earned him the nickname of 'the boy wonder', but it is a fair assessment of his talents as an inside man. Certainly, McGrory, his chief beneficiary, was full of praise for the play of McInally.

Maley himself, up to his death in 1958, retained his romantic belief in the brilliance of Tommy. Bob McPhail was of the opinion that Maley loved Tommy but was scared to admit it, even to himself. He certainly overlooked Tommy's indiscretions time and time again. Maley, himself the son of a soldier and very strictly brought up, possibly felt that he might have liked to have himself been a little wilder in his youth. Perhaps he might have wished he had sown a few wild oats before becoming the dignified, austere Mr. Celtic. Robert Burns perhaps sums up Maley's type:

> Ye are sae grave, nae doot yer wise
> And fairly though ye do despise
> The hairum-scairum ram-stam boys
> The rattlin' squad
> I note ye upward cast yer eyes
> Ye ken the road!

One night in the 1950s Maley, by this time an old

man, was interviewed by a journalist about his career and life in football, and talked at length about the many brilliant players, like McMahon, Quinn, Young, Gallacher, McGrory and Delaney, that he had seen at Celtic Park. When pressed as to who was the greatest of them all (and in truth, it was an impressive list of talent), Maley stopped, looked at his interlocutor, then turned his gaze into the coal fire burning merrily away, then looked at the man again and said, 'The greatest? Why, that was Tom McInally.'

Other assessments of Tommy are less kind. *An Alphabet of the Celts* (MacBride, O'Connor and Sheridan) says 'In fact, he achieved relatively little' in proportion to the amount of talent he had, and to the expectations of his adoring public. And Tom Campbell, in his biography of *Charlie Tully – Celtic's Cheeky Chappie*, compares Tully and McInally, where there were indeed great similarities, but concludes that, whereas Tully could play the clown on occasion, McInally *was* a clown. Jim Craig, the Lisbon Lion, in *A Lion Looks Back*, is quite succinct about McInally: 'a genius but not a worker'.

John Cairney, in his excellent *Heroes Are Forever* biography of Jimmy McGrory, sums up McInally thus:

> Tommy was his own worst enemy – and he eventually killed the genius that everyone knew was in him. Maley indulged him to the limit. He knew what he had on his hands, but Tommy went his own way – downhill. Latterly he refused to train. He didn't need a manager, he needed a psychiatrist. Inevitably he hit the bottle. One has only to think of George Best's liver troubles. Or George Connelly's psychological problems in a later Celtic. Prodigious talent – prodigally thrown away.

192

There are of course all sorts of salutary lessons to be learned from Tommy's life, and young footballers would do well to heed them. But there is something very archetypically Scottish about having talent and failing to cope with it. The number of Scottish footballers who have hit the self-destruct button are legend. Hughie Gallacher got further than McInally in the game, but destroyed himself far more spectacularly by throwing himself off a railway bridge while facing a charge of child neglect. Jimmy Johnstone, as he himself cheerfully admitted, would have fizzled out of the game in a cloud of alcoholism if it hadn't been for 'Big Jock'. Genius and the Scottish character do not always go well together.

One of the paradoxes often said about Tommy (and indeed it has been said about George Best, Maradona, Jimmy Johnstone and others) is that 'if he hadn't been such a great player, he could have been even better'. At first, this sounds absurd, but what is meant is that Tommy was such a supremely talented player that he felt that he did not need to bother training and taking himself seriously. He was anything but the supremely dedicated professional that we have seen in Kenny Dalglish and Henrik Larsson, as well as in countless others of lesser ability. Had he only behaved himself, he might have taken Celtic to unbelievable heights of success and prolonged his own career by many more years. For youngsters reading this, there is no end of a lesson here.

We have seen many players of undoubted talent who have fallen down for one reason or another. Jock Stein, for example, was once asked who was the best player he had ever had dealings with. To everyone's surprise, he did not say Johnstone or McNeill or Murdoch or Tully but a chap called Willie Hamilton, whom he had managed with Hibs in 1964. Willie had loads of talent but is now an obscure character because he could not cope with the demands of professional football off the field. And then there was Chic Charnley, a man of several clubs in the 1980s and 1990s – Clydebank, Partick Thistle, St. Mirren, Hibs. He also was extremely gifted, but failed to toe the line. It was a shame that he never got the move to Celtic that he craved, but there were possibly reasons for this.

Tommy McInally would not have been the character that he was without the clowning. Even in his post-playing days, he was always telling jokes, acting the fool and impressing youngsters. Everyone loved him. Any enemies that he may have made were forgiven and forgotten about. He was reconciled to his old mentor Willie Maley whom he would visit and talk endlessly about football and Celtic. It is interesting that his death notice in *The Glasgow Herald* said that he was 'ex-Celtic', without any mention of his time with Third Lanark or with Sunderland. These were almost irrelevant to the memory of Tommy, who was linked inextricably with Celtic, for he was very much a Celtic character and legend. It is just a shame that Tommy did not always do what he could have for Celtic and their supporters. But then again, if he had always behaved, never smoked or drunk, never argued with authority, never disputed a referee's decision, never been anything other than a model professional – then he would not have been Tommy McInally!